LESSONS
FROM
GOD

Keys for Living a Victorious Life

TANYA VEZZA

Lessons From God - Copyright © 2018 - Tanya Vezza

This book is copyrighted by Tanya Vezza. All rights reserved.

No part of this publication may be reproduced, stored in a retrieval system or transmitted in any way by any means, electronic, mechanical, photocopy, recording, or otherwise, without the prior permission of the author except as provided by USA copyright law.

Cover designed by germancreative – Fiverr.

Edited by Lisa Thompson at www.writebylisa.com. You can email Lisa at writebylisa@gmail.com for your editing needs.

Formatting by Rik – www.WildSeasFormatting.com.

Scripture quotations marked (NIV) are taken from the Holy Bible, New International Version®, NIV®. Copyright © 1973, 1978, 1984, 2011 by Biblica, Inc.™ Used by permission of Zondervan. All rights reserved worldwide. www.zondervan.com The "NIV" and "New International Version" are trademarks registered in the United States Patent and Trademark Office by Biblica, Inc.™

Scripture quotations marked (NLT) are taken from the New Living Translation. Holy Bible, New Living Translation, copyright © 1996, 2004, 2015 by Tyndale House Foundation. Used by permission of Tyndale House Publishers Inc., Carol Stream, Illinois 60188. All rights reserved.

Scripture quotations marked (NASB) are taken from the New American Standard Bible®, Copyright © 1960, 1962, 1963, 1968, 1971, 1972, 1973, 1975, 1977, 1995 by The Lockman Foundation. Used by permission. www.Lockman.org

Scripture quotations marked (MSG) are taken from THE MESSAGE, copyright © 1993, 1994, 1995, 1996, 2000, 2001, 2002 by Eugene H. Peterson. Used by permission of NavPress. All rights reserved. Represented by Tyndale House Publishers, Inc.

Scripture quotations marked (NKJV) are taken from the New King James Version. Copyright © 1982 by Thomas Nelson, Inc. Used by permission. All rights reserved.

Content from *Lessons from God: Keys for Living a Victorious Life*, Lesson Four: Communication, was originally printed in *God Speaks: Perspectives on Hearing God's Voice*, by Praying Medic, published by Inkity Press, 2017.

Paperback: ISBN: 978-0-9995566-0-3
Ebook: ISBN: 978-0-9995566-1-0

For my husband and children, whose love and support helped make this book possible.

With thanks to my parents, who encouraged me to write and taught me that anything was possible.

TABLE OF CONTENTS

INTRODUCTION vii
LESSON 1: BELIEVE 1
LESSON 2: FOLLOW 21
LESSON 3: TRUST 41
LESSON 4: COMMUNICATE 63
LESSON 5: WARRIOR 79
LESSON 6: OVERCOME 91
LESSON 7: GRACE 105

INTRODUCTION

A COUPLE OF YEARS AGO, the Lord began the process of placing key elements of living in His freedom on my heart. I felt a nudge to more fully explore how the Lord has used these keys to change and shape my life for the better. As I studied their impact on my life, I also began to see parallels in the Bible and in the lives of powerful Christians throughout history.

These key tools are the result of lessons I've learned from the Lord over the course of my life. Every lesson came out of working with the Lord through many life experiences and various circumstances. Each situation revealed a new facet of the Lord's character and heart.

The Lord truly desires for us to live in His victory and freedom. These fundamental elements of relationship with Him are the building blocks to create that life. Following these keys will transform you and set you free in every area of your life. They will also empower you and unleash your God-given creative abilities.

A quote from my daughter best summarizes the central theme expressed throughout this work. Simply stated, "As children of God, there comes a time when He begins to prepare us for greatness. We discover how God speaks to us and mentors us in ways that we learn timeless lessons that shape us into the warriors of tomorrow." (Emily Vezza, paraphrased)

LESSON 1: BELIEVE

WHAT IF WE TOOK GOD at His Word? What if we truly believed that all of the seemingly impossible promises the Lord has made to us are actually already ours? What if we believed that, just like Jesus, we, too, are endowed with the same powers and abilities to perform miracles? Think of how our lives and those of the people around us would be transformed as a result of such radical belief.

A great awakening is happening throughout the earth as people are beginning to accept and embrace a God that cannot and will not be contained within the walls of a building one day of the week or in the box in which people try to put Him so that they can feel comfortable. A restlessness groans in creation, a yearning for the true expression of God in all His glory and splendor. A remnant hungers and thirsts for the freedom that only the Lord can provide.

Out of love for His creation, the Lord has chosen such a time as this to awaken us to the things we have forgotten. We have forgotten the very nature and essence of who God is and that we are created in His image. We have forgotten the immense power of simple, childlike belief in Him. We have forgotten that, through Christ, we have been given a limitless inheritance. We have forgotten that we are sons and daughters of a King, endowed with His power and abilities. We have forgotten that we have been set free to transform this world into the Kingdom that God has always intended.

Simply Believe

Several years ago, the Lord started putting the following Scripture verse on my heart, "I tell you the truth, anyone who believes in me will do the same works I have done, and even greater works, because I am going to be with the Father" (John 14:12, NLT). He kept asking me to ponder this deeply, and I felt His urge to believe that this is truly possible. He repeatedly emphasized, "Anyone who believes will do the same things as Jesus and even greater works."

I went on long prayer walks with the Lord, repeating this over and over again in my mind, until, one day, in the middle of my prayer walk, it finally hit me.

I am one of the people who will do greater things than Jesus did on this earth.

For years, the Lord had me ponder this promise until it became so deeply ingrained in me that I knew with every fiber of my being that it was true and that it applied to me. It applies to everyone who will take it to heart and believe that not only is it true but that they will come to see it come to pass in their lives.

Take a look at the life of Peter as an example of someone who believed and saw his life transformed as a result. In Acts, it says, "As a result of the apostles' work, sick people were brought out into the streets on beds and mats so that Peter's shadow might fall across some of them as he went by" (Acts 5:15, NLT). Peter understood his place in and with the Father to such a degree that he simply had to be present and the sick were healed. He didn't need to know who was sick or what they were suffering from. He didn't need to speak or to conjure up the strength to heal. Without effort, even his shadow healed.

In a similar account of Paul in Acts, he was ministering in Ephesus and God gave him power to perform unusual miracles. "When handkerchiefs or aprons that had merely touched his skin were placed on sick people, they were healed of their diseases, and evil spirits were expelled" (Acts 19:12, NLT). Peter and Paul operated out of their place of authority in the Lord. Just as when Jesus healed the Roman officer's slave, they did not need to be physically present for the power of their authority in Christ to change the situation and bring forth healing. The God-like abilities shown in Peter and Paul stemmed from a simple but firm belief in the promises God made to them and by operating out of the power that their faith activated.

Our simple, childlike faith activates the incredible gifts that God has placed inside His people. Unfortunately, a long time ago in church history, an idea planted by the enemy infiltrated our theology and beliefs about God's gifts. That idea was that miracles and gifts, such as healing and prophecy, were specifically designed for Jesus' time and that, a short time later, those gifts ceased to exist. Over time, people stopped believing in the gifts of the Spirit. Ultimately, the enemy was able to so deceive people that these gifts from God became viewed as of the devil. As a result, miracles and the gifts of God became less prevalent. People simply stopped exercising these gifts because they believed or were told that they no longer existed or were inherently bad.

Why would the enemy be so concerned about these gifts? Because he knows that if we use these God-given gifts, we will change the world. When Jesus was sacrificed on our behalf, God the Father stripped all of the devil's power from Him. He is powerless. The only power he has over us is the power we give him. We give him power when we believe his lies. By submitting to the lie that we were essentially powerless, the enemy was able to subdue an immensely powerful army of God's people for many centuries.

The enemy knows that we are more powerful than he is. He is utterly afraid of God's people and what he knows we are capable of doing if we simply believe. When we perform miracles and operate in all the gifts of the Holy Spirit, we derail and dismantle the enemy. He cannot fight against the gifts of God.

Jesus shared a story about God's nature as Father. "Which of you, if your son asks for bread, will give him a stone? Or if he asks for a fish, will give him a snake? If you, then, though you are evil, know how to give good gifts to your children, how much more will your Father in heaven give good gifts to those who ask him!" (Matthew 7:9-11, NIV). The best gift that our Father gave us was the Holy Spirit. With that gift, He enabled and empowered us to do His will in the Earth. He gave us the "authority to trample on snakes and scorpions and to overcome all the power of the enemy," and promised, "nothing will harm you" (Luke 10:19, NIV). What good and perfect Father would give us that gift and then take it away? He wouldn't, and He didn't!

His gift of power through the Holy Spirit is available to His children for all eternity. We simply need to believe again and regain what is rightfully ours in Christ. What gifts are we squelching through fear or unbelief? How would our lives improve if we allowed God's promises to transform us?

These words are causing fear to rise up in some who are reading this. I can completely understand and relate to this. Stepping out of the realm of the norm is being willing to be seen as different. It is coming out of a large flock of fearful sheep with a light shining on us. We can no longer hide among the masses. Once we step out, we cannot go back. Our actions might incite ridicule and confusion among those we hold dear. But there comes a place in our walk with the Lord where the fear of staying trapped where we are outweighs the fear of change. And that is when change occurs.

Freedom is not free. A cost is always involved. But the cost is nothing when compared to the abundant and victorious life that awaits us. Believing and trusting in God's promises will completely transform our lives and empower us. God is giving us permission, and all of heaven is cheering us on to become the miracle and the gift we are meant to be in this earth! Simply believe.

Our Inheritance

The inheritance we received when Jesus died is that God imparted all of the power that was in His Son to us. Jesus taught us that His power was from God and part of God, and that, like Him, we are one with God. God has entrusted us with His power and taken up residence inside His people. All of God's power and creative ability is available to us to use.

Jesus even referred to us as God, saying, "Is it not written in your Law, 'I have said you are "gods"'" (John 10:34, NIV). Most people don't take God at His word. If He has said, "you are 'gods,'" then He has made us to be as God and to rule with Him just as Jesus does.

God has endowed us with His power and creative abilities because He trusts us. Jesus told His disciples, "I no longer call you servants, because a servant does not know his master's business. Instead, I have called you friends, for everything that I learned from my Father I have made known to you" (John 15:15, NIV). He shared everything that His Father showed Him with His disciples. Jesus clearly modeled a life of doing only what His Father showed Him. This means that God intended to show the people He created how to fully and freely operate in His power.

God is calling us His friends. God is showing us immense trust and faith. He is trusting us with this power because He knows that only those who will dare to believe they have the power of God living inside them will actually activate, through their faith, the inheritance that was given to all of God's children through Christ. Sadly, due to fear or religion or misguided theology, most people live their entire lives suppressing their God-given birthright.

Because we, like Jesus, are now one with the Father, when we speak, we speak from a place of authority and with the creative power of God. The Lord, speaking through the prophet Isaiah, declared, "So is my word that goes out from my mouth: It will not return to me empty, but will accomplish what I desire and achieve the purpose for which I sent it" (Isaiah 55:11, NIV). We are speaking God's will and His words when we speak in accordance with the Holy Spirit's leading. God's Word will not come back void, which means that, when we speak with His wisdom and authority, we are now co-creators with Him.

I do not think that most children of God realize the incredible creative abilities that are released through them when they speak. Genesis says, "In the beginning God created the heavens and the earth. Now the earth was formless and empty, darkness was over the surface of the deep, and the Spirit of God was hovering over the waters. And God said, 'Let there be light,' and there was light" (Genesis 1:1-3, NIV). God's spoken word created the heavens and the earth.

The power to create or destroy comes from the words we speak. The Bible states that we have the power of life and death in our words. Proverbs 18:21 clearly says, "The tongue can bring death or life; those who love to talk will reap the consequences" (NLT). God has given us authority, so when we speak, a divine command is being spoken. When we speak, we release angels and other heavenly hosts to bring into existence the very things that we have spoken.

Have you ever noticed that negative people who only speak about how bad everything is in their life end up leading miserable lives? These people are unwittingly or unknowingly speaking "death" over their lives. Positive people, who speak words filled with optimism and hope, are speaking "life" over themselves and end up leading happier, more successful lives. Our words and our thoughts create our reality.

An integral link connects what we think and the words we speak to express those thoughts. What we think ultimately becomes integrated into our heart, which is the core of our being. This correlation is clearly stated in the Bible in the following passage. "For the mouth speaks what the heart is full of. A good man brings good things out of the good stored up in him, and an evil man brings evil things out of the evil stored up in him" (Matthew 12:34b-35, NIV).

The Lord often uses prophetic promises, in part, to help us think bigger and envision a better future for ourselves. The promise God spoke to Abraham is one such example as recorded in Hebrews. "When God made his promise to Abraham, since there was no one greater for him to swear by, he swore by himself, saying, 'I will surely bless you and give you many descendants.' And so after waiting patiently, Abraham received what was promised" (Hebrews 6:13-15, NIV). God's spoken promise helped Abraham to start believing that he would have a better life and the desire of his heart, a child. The onus to fulfill the promise was God's. Abraham's part was to trust God's promise and hold on to it until it manifested in his life.

What we focus on becomes bigger and more powerful in our minds. When we think on something long enough, it becomes part of us. Eventually, we act out on those thoughts through our words or actions. When we speak the things in our hearts, we are prophesying over ourselves. If we are going to prophesy our future, we need to make sure it is filled with life and what the Lord desires for us.

Not every thought that enters our minds is from God. Just as with spirits, we must test the thoughts that come to us. If they are not filled with life and hope, they are not from the Lord. If they produce fear or a sense of urgency, again, they are not from God. The thoughts that are truly from God will be consistent with His recorded Word. You will know a thing is from God, no matter how much it might or might not make sense to you in the natural, when it produces a sense of peace and joy that could only come from Him. Those are the thoughts that we think on until they become a part of us.

When what we focus on brings us to a place of such belief that we speak it out in faith, we will elicit heavenly and demonic responses. The dark forces of this earth will be in abject fear the instant we begin to speak out and exercise our authority. They will try to bring about distractions in the natural to dissuade us from continuing. Through our circumstances, the enemy will try to bring about a fear that will cause us to stop.

In those moments when we feel hemmed in and at our breaking point, continue pressing forward. When we don't see a way through, we must keep speaking the words that God has given to us as His promise for our lives. When we believe in our heart and declare with our mouth the very things that God has spoken to us for our lives, we unleash the power of God to bring those very things to fruition. We stand on and declare the truth that God has spoken to us until it becomes a reality in the natural.

God's children are becoming aware of their true inheritance and rightful place in His Kingdom. The words we use determine the degree to which we live out that legacy. What if, at this special time in history, the Lord wants us to speak new words? Words that bring healing to nations. Words that solve critical problems. Words that create peace. Words that help usher in His Kingdom.

I encourage you to spend some quiet time with the Lord. Ask Him what He wants you to be speaking. This might be something specific over your life or a realm where you have authority, such as a spiritual region or a nation. You might discover that He has given you authority to speak healing or against natural disasters or any number of amazing things. In addition, ask Him what specific gifts are part of your inheritance and how you can partner with Him to use them to their fullest potential.

Sons and Daughters

Now is an exceptionally unique time in history. The sons and daughters of God are being revealed in the earth to do His good will and to advance the Kingdom of God. Now is the time to release the Kingdom of God on the earth. Jesus prayed, "Your kingdom come, your will be done, on earth as it is in heaven"(Matthew 6:10, NIV). The will of God for His creation is His Kingdom revealed and set free in the earth. It is time to manifest the expression of God's love through His Kingdom and through His sons and daughters. It is time for the sons and daughters of God to wake up the remnant left in the earth.

And who are these sons and daughters of God? They are a people who have chosen God above everything else in this world and at great cost to themselves. God had called and chosen them well before the foundations of the earth for this specific time. He created each one to carry a part of His Kingdom that only they are uniquely gifted to reveal and bring forth in the earth. They are His song of love to an earth that has been groaning and crying out to be restored to its former glory. Yes, His sons and daughters can actually hear and feel the earth's groaning.

They have been hidden and protected under God's wings while God has trained them. And I assure you, this is a training that most would have refused. Because of the weight of their calling, nothing but God can be in them. They had to be willing to submit themselves to God to such a degree that He could purge every impurity out of them through His all-consuming fire. Out of love for them and the earth and all of His creation, He had to fully prepare His beloved to successfully bring forth the Kingdom of God on this earth.

Under the shadow of God's wings and protection, many have been hidden away from the world, undergoing training for decades. Every false system of this world, of men, and of the enemy must be revealed and removed. When we are born and raised in a truly Matrix-like world, we are often unaware that almost everything we were taught or learned growing up is not part of God's intention for His creation and does not originate from Him.

When they said "yes" to their training, some of God's sons and daughters were stripped of everything. They lost their good names, reputations, sense of security, finances, bearings, friends, jobs, sometimes their health, and in some instances, their joy and hope. They were subjected to tests and trials in unending waves for decades.

They clung to God in the midst of their trials because He was all that was left in their lives. However, their outer circumstances portrayed an image that they were the most utter of failures. To those on the outside, they appeared as if they were somehow being punished by God for their incorrect theology and crazy beliefs about Him. They were openly and secretly ridiculed by friends, families, and strangers. For up to a decade or more, they were tested past the point of breaking, till even after everything they had withstood, they were not sure they could last a moment longer. In obscurity, they experienced the same trials and tribulations as Jesus.

As painful and difficult as the training was, it was very necessary. God had to fully prepare His sons and daughters. He had to completely strip them down to nothing and then completely rebuild them in His truth and light. This passage illustrates this principle, "But he who practices the truth comes to the Light, so that his deeds may be manifested as having been wrought in God" (John 3:21, NASB).

Throughout history, God has always prepared and equipped His chosen people for the time in which they are living. God never starts a work that He has not already completed in heaven. He has chosen this moment in time and His sons and daughters to bring forth His Kingdom on earth. He invested the time and training necessary to properly train His Bride for the victory that He has already secured.

The time of training has ended, and it is time for the sons and daughters of God to be revealed. How will they be recognized? In Matthew 5:14-16, it says, "You are the light of the world. A town built on a hill cannot be hidden. Neither do people light a lamp and put it under a bowl. Instead they put it on its stand, and it gives light to everyone in the house. In the same way, let your light shine before others, that they may see your good deeds and glorify your Father in heaven" (NIV). They will operate from a place of authority as demonstrated in their words and actions. The things and cares of this world will not affect the sons and daughters in any manner. They will walk and operate in freedom.

God's chosen ones, His Bride, will be completely set apart. You will be able to sense and feel the presence of the Lord within them. Signs and wonders, miracles, and the supernatural will accompany them. The supernatural is the natural state of being for the one who walks with God. The supernatural occurrences that naturally flow out of the sons and daughters will be a part of their everyday lives.

This will be so evident that, when you see them, something in your spirit will confirm that they are special. When they walk into a room, their anointing will enter first; people will take notice and realize that they are important in God's Kingdom. The sons and daughters will speak from a place of authority, and the people who hear them will recognize that and pay attention to their words.

The sons and daughters of God will have immense creative abilities. The authority of their spoken words will cause the things they speak to become reality. Through their creative gifts, they will be able to call forth the unseen into being. They will speak over nations, declaring God's will for that region, and see it come to pass. Leaders of nations, those with power and wealth, even kings and queens, will seek out the counsel of the sons and daughters. The wisdom deposited in them by God will bring forth solutions to seemingly impossible situations in the world.

Their greatest collective gift to the earth will be to usher forth the Kingdom of God. Through their words, thoughts, and deeds they will embody "on earth as it is in heaven." Through the example of their lives, they will represent the Kingdom of God and how it operates.

The Kingdom of God is hard to express in human terms. It is not a system as systems come from man, and God operates outside of man's understanding and natural abilities. Man's systems, such as governments, politics, religion, economics, and so on, are all inherently flawed because they originate from man. All systems are set up to benefit a certain subset of people while excluding or hindering others. Manmade systems are also designed to enrich a small, special group of people at the top while depleting the resources of the much larger group of the common, everyday person.

All of man's systems operate from a mindset of lack. In basic terms, this premise believes that there are a limited or finite amount of resources in the earth. People who operate from lack feel the need to hoard. They have a fear-based need to acquire as many resources as possible for themselves whatever the cost. They want to make sure that they are not left out when the resources run out. They basically have a "take-care-of-my-own" mentality.

The Kingdom does not operate this way. God's Kingdom flows out of a state of abundance. God's will is for all of His children to thrive. His Son came to give us life and life abundantly. God desires for all of His children to live in a state of plenty, and He has supplied more than enough resources for everyone to do so.

In fact, He has vast treasure troves of resources that He is willing to release into the earth. The storehouses of heaven are immense and barely tapped. God also fully has the ability to supernaturally create more of a particular resource or to create an entirely new and better resource if that resource were depleted. Man restricts God's graciousness and care and love for His children by trying to confine Him to the limited abilities of what they can comprehend or see with their natural eyes.

His Kingdom on earth will operate according to these principles when the sons and daughters of God establish it on earth. In the Kingdom of God, there is plenty. In the Kingdom of God, all thrive and flourish. In the Kingdom of God, there is cooperation for the greater good. In the Kingdom of God, there is peace and joy. In the Kingdom of God, His children are part of a royal priesthood. In the Kingdom of God, people only do what they see the Father doing, just as Christ did. Truly, the Kingdom of God is beyond description. It cannot be fully expressed through human means or words.

Set Free

When I was a teenager, the Lord showed me a vision that contained a couple of scenes. In the vision, I saw myself grown up and married with two preteen children, the older a girl and the younger a boy.

In the first scene, we were eating in a restaurant. I could somewhat hear the conversations of people sitting near our table. As far as I could tell, most of them were in difficult situations. My heart went out to them. A short time later, we finished our meal, paid, and started walking toward the door. Near the door, sitting at a counter, a weary-looking woman sat with two small children. They were quietly and happily eating their food. She had a cup of black coffee in front of her that was barely touched, and she appeared to be wringing her hands. I had the impression that she was struggling financially. I also felt that she wasn't sure if she even had enough money to pay for their meal. The instant I stepped past this woman, money appeared in front of her on the counter—dollar bills and gold coins. The glint of the coins caused me to look her direction. As my husband opened the door for us, I heard the excited and happy voices of the people I had overhead while we were eating. All of the problems they were facing had suddenly disappeared or were corrected. The most memorable incident was a couple whose phone rang as we were leaving. A family member who lived in another location was seriously ill and had taken a turn for the worse. I had the impression that their loved one was terminally ill. Their family had called to tell them that the sick family member had miraculously been healed. They had tears of joy streaming down their faces as they hugged each other, and they started jumping up and down in the restaurant, praising God. We walked through the door of the restaurant. As the door shut behind us, I was immediately launched into the next scene.

In the second scene, our family was walking down the sidewalk on a beautiful day with comfortable temperatures and a clear blue sky with billowy white clouds. We were in a part of town where most families struggle to make ends meet. Our family was talking, laughing, and enjoying each other's company as we walked. I noticed that certain people seemed drawn to us. In one case, a young man was walking toward us but on the other side of the street. He crossed the street to come and talk to us. As soon as he was in front of us, our spirits knew what he needed. We started talking, and the Lord orchestrated our conversation in a free-flowing manner. He mentioned that there was something different about our family and said that he could feel, sense, and see something special around us, which had drawn him to us. He felt that we had what his heart had been searching and longing for. We spoke exactly what the Lord put on our hearts to share with him. In the midst of talking to him, his eyes grew big, and a smile covered his face. He had been searching for a powerful relationship with the Lord like his spirit recognized in our family. He connected with something the Lord had us share with him, and his face lit up. He thanked us and went on his way. We continued walking, only this time, I noticed people giving us strange looks. Instead of coming toward us, some people were walking away from us, even crossing the street to avoid us with wary or even scared looks on their faces. I was confused and couldn't understand why people would be afraid of us or treat us that way. Then, I had the sense to not worry about it and to just keep walking. We continued walking, and the vision ended.

Over the years, I have revisited this vision with the Lord. I believe He has shown me that the significance of the first scene relates to living our lives in such a place of connection and intimacy with God that, like Peter, miracles occur when we walk by people. Or like Paul, people are healed even if they aren't physically present simply when we hear that someone is sick.

We don't even have to think about causing a miracle for it to manifest in the natural. The God in us is fully integrated in our lives, naturally releasing the miraculous through us when our spirit recognizes a need. The Lord showed this in operation in my vision when the money supernaturally appeared and when the terminally ill person was healed in another city. The people in my vision never verbalized their needs or asked me for help, yet the very things they needed were provided by my presence.

I believe this is similar in principle to the healing of the woman with the issue of blood. Her story is told in Matthew 9:20-21, "Just then a woman who had been subject to bleeding for twelve years came up behind him and touched the edge of his cloak. She said to herself, 'If I only touch his cloak, I will be healed'" (NIV). Additional details follow in Luke 8:45-46 and 48, "'Who touched me?' Jesus asked. When they all denied it, Peter said, 'Master, the people are crowding and pressing against you.' But Jesus said, 'Someone touched me; I know that power has gone out from me' . . . . Then he said to her, 'Daughter, your faith has healed you. Go in peace'" (NIV).

The woman understood that all she had to do was access the presence of Jesus to be healed. He didn't even know what she needed but as soon as she touched Him, healing power instantly came out of Him to help her. Jesus helped and healed all who came to Him. The nature of God is to restore. One needs merely to come in contact with someone like Peter or Paul or you or me, and the power of God within us will provide what their needy spirit is crying out for via a transaction of spirit to spirit.

I believe the second scene of my vision refers to the fact that the sons and daughters of God are set apart. In 1 Peter 2:9, they are described as "a chosen people, a royal priesthood, a holy nation, God's special possession, that you may declare the praises of him who called you out of darkness into his wonderful light" (NIV). The calling of God on these people's lives is so distinct and palpable that anyone who comes in contact with them can sense and feel that they are different.

Like the young man in my vision, some people will be drawn to us because their spirit recognizes that we possess what they are searching for or need. The people in my vision who were scared of us or repelled by our presence were not ready to change; they recognized the light inside of us but were not ready to allow that light to dispel the dark places in them. God never forces us to change, so I believe that is why He instructed us to just keep walking. He knew it wasn't the right timing during this encounter; however, I do believe that in the future, He could use the memory of our brief meeting to help change those people's lives for the better. It is the Holy Spirit's job to reveal the Father; it is my job to do whatever the Father asks of me and leave the outcome to

Him. He is extremely good at using a seemingly failed encounter to plant a seed for a future date.

While the people in the vision were my family, I believe the Lord was using us as an archetypal representation for all His children. Just like Peter and Paul, we represented people changed into the image of Christ through His transformative work in our lives. This powerful life is not just for a few but is God's design for all His children. God's people are at the very heart and core of His Kingdom. And His Kingdom is at hand.

LESSON 2: FOLLOW

SO OFTEN, WE THINK OF following the Lord in terms of what makes us comfortable. In reality, He wants so much more for us. The breakthrough, the healing we need, the next level in our journey, and the huge achievements that the Lord desires for us are way beyond our current comfort level.

Most people believe that God wouldn't put His people in situations that upset us, cause us pain, hurt our feelings, or challenge us. What kind of a powerful and loving God does that? What perfect Heavenly Father would allow a single child of His to stay trapped in the pain of their past hurts, wrong mindsets, destructive patterns, and limiting beliefs?

The difference is in our perspective. We see things from a worldly and temporal mindset. On the other hand, the Lord views situations from His side of eternity and a mindset that is higher than human reasoning. Our view is usually so narrow that we miss the bigger picture and settle for less than what God desires to give us. God always thinks bigger and wants better for us than we could ever dream. We must let go of our desires, trust in God, and follow His leading. The Lord invites each of us on an epic journey that includes: action on our part, a trek through the wilderness, transformation, and redemption. However, this journey lies on the other side of our comfort and fears.

Action

Lao Tzu coined a common yet inspiring quote: "Every journey begins with a single step."[1] Any journey in life begins with the simple action of deciding to take the very first step necessary to embark upon a new venture, and this first step requires faith. A journey might relate to a physical journey or an emotional or spiritual journey, such as taking control of your health, overcoming a bad habit, working on that difficult relationship, or moving across the country. No two journeys are alike; however, all journeys start with the action of daring to venture into the unknown. Paradoxically, the first step is usually relatively easy in nature yet, at the same time, dauntingly difficult to actually take. Envisioning a new venture is challenging enough let alone acting upon those thoughts or promptings from the Lord.

When we risk moving forward from the safety and comfort of the known, we face our fears. We are willing to be stretched and challenged in order to grow and evolve into that which we long to experience or become. We make a conscious choice to risk failure in the pursuit of what others consider merely a dream. By taking that first step, we ultimately refuse to continue settling for less than God's best for our lives.

The reason this first step is so difficult for many is that it involves a leap of faith. So often, God's people expect Him to show them everything with all the plans

---

[1] *BBC – Learning English*. 2009. "Learning English – Moving Words – Lao Tzu."
http://www.bbc.co.uk/worldservice/learningenglish/movingwords/shortlist/laotzu.shtml.

perfectly laid out before they are willing to start. However, the Lord doesn't work that way. He requires that we take the first step, and then, He shows us the next part of His plan.

Even as I write this, I am in the midst of walking by faith. A year ago, the Lord asked our family to leave a comfortable life and move halfway across the country. Nothing could have prepared us for what we've experienced over this past year in this journey. Our family is completely dependent on the Lord's leading and guiding because we have no idea where we are going or what the next step is that we need to take. We are walking blindly. Even so, we are standing in a position of trust that the Lord still has our best interests at heart and that He will lead us to where He knows is best.

The Lord leads His people in this manner for strategic reasons. If we're completely honest with ourselves, if we knew the entire game plan from the beginning, we would have no need for trust or faith. Also, we would likely question and doubt God's plan because it wouldn't make any sense to us. We would ultimately get in His way, slow things down, and cause problems. Finally, we would unwittingly divulge valuable information to the enemy about God's plan for our lives.

While I know that the devil has been destroyed and his power has been stripped from him, he persists as if he still has power. The only real access he has in any believer's life is that which we give him by believing his lies, which is the only weapon he has left at his disposal. I have no desire to give the enemy any kind of information that he would try to twist or use against me.

A spiritual war has been waging since the beginning of time. Within that war are two opposing armies, each with their own general at the helm. God, our supreme leader, is our general and mastermind of plans and tactics, and the devil is the general of the opposition.

The most successful tactics in maneuvering to overcome one's adversary include attacking where the enemy is unprepared and unable to recover as well as unexpected appearance or movement. A key strategy of any successful general is secrecy and surprise. This tactic is clearly outlined in *The Art of War*, "Thus a skillful general conducts his army just as if he were leading a single man, willy-nilly by the hand. It is the business of a general to be serene and inscrutable, impartial and self-controlled. He should be capable of keeping his officers and men in ignorance of his plans. He changes his methods and alters his plans so that people have no knowledge of what he aims at."[2]

In an act of supreme love, the Lord hides information from us that we do not need to know or are incapable of understanding now. This brilliant strategy ensures victory for His beloved. When we only know the present movement, the enemy has absolutely no way to gain a tactical advantage against us.

A great example of someone who followed the leading of the Lord is Abraham. In Genesis, the Lord tells Abram:

"Go from your country, your people and your father's household to the land I will show you.

---

[2] Tzu, Sun. 1998. *The Art of War*. Hertfordshire, England: Wordsworth Editions Limited.

"I will make you into a great nation,
and I will bless you;
I will make your name great,
and you will be a blessing.
I will bless those who bless you,
and whoever curses you I will curse;
and all peoples on earth
will be blessed through you."

So Abram went, as the LORD had told him (Genesis 12:1-4, NIV).

The first thing God does is to ask Abram to trust Him. The very next thing He does is make Abram a promise. Then, the Lord sends Abram off into the wilderness where He can change him into Abraham. God always operates in this manner. Before the Lord ever asks anyone to embark on a journey, He first secures their victory in heaven. When God makes His promise to Abram, He is speaking out the future that He has already obtained. The Lord prophesies our future to help elevate us to the next level while, at the same time, opening our eyes to a hidden gift He has placed inside us. He also knows that, during the testing of the wilderness, we will need to hold on to that promise in order to keep going.

Wilderness

The next step in this epic journey is a wilderness experience. We have successfully overcome our fears and taken the first step. The Lord encourages us and starts revealing the next step each time we move forward in faith. However, at some mysterious point in our fledgling journey, the euphoria wears off; we take our eyes off the road, and we realize that we have no idea where we are or where we're headed. We also discover at this point that the Lord isn't supplying our needs as quickly as He did at the beginning of our journey.

The Lord works incrementally in our lives. Just as children must learn to walk before they can run, the Lord must build a solid foundation in our lives before we can successfully carry out the destiny that He has for us. This process is explained in Romans 8:29-30a, "God knew what he was doing from the very beginning. He decided from the outset to shape the lives of those who love him along the same lines as the life of his Son" (MSG). He must fully prepare us at each stage of the journey to handle the next level of our calling.

The first step of our journey required overt and timely acts of His faithfulness. However, if we stayed there, we would remain dependent infants. At some point, we must all grow up biologically and spiritually, and that process is often uncomfortable. In the wilderness, the Lord stretches us beyond what we feel capable of enduring. In the wilderness, we are plagued with challenges and delays.

Abram faced many difficulties in the wilderness. One of the first challenges he faced was a famine that led him to

Egypt. Out of fear for his life, Abram lied to Pharaoh about his wife to protect himself. Clearly, Abram failed miserably at this first testing of his faith. However, the Lord did not respond to him based on his failure but on the potential still hidden deep inside. God knew who Abram truly was and his real nature better than he did. Not only did the Lord keep Pharaoh from touching Abram's wife, He compelled the ruler of Egypt to richly bless Abram financially. What I love about this experience is the fact that Abram made the same mistake a second time, and God's response to him was exactly the same in both instances.

The Lord is extremely patient. He is more concerned with the journey and the process of molding His children than with the final product. The purpose of the wilderness is not performance but the conscious act on our parts of submitting to the Lord's desires for our lives and yielding our will to His in order to allow Him to make the necessary changes in our character. On our part, we must be willing to stand and continue to stand as the Lord consumes us with His fire to burn off the impurities. However, we know that we will fail in the process. Even so, the mistakes we make are actually part of our learning process, and ultimately, the Lord will use these mistakes to help us.

In the midst of the muck and mess of the wilderness, you can easily look at your circumstances and start questioning whether you correctly heard the Lord. If you did hear accurately, you start wondering what you are doing wrong to produce the results you're experiencing. To be honest, at some points in this part of the journey, it is difficult not to question and second guess what's happening because circumstances are so chaotic. So many things often seem to go wrong, and your life no longer makes any sense.

Can you imagine how Joseph felt during his thirteen years in the wilderness? He found himself stripped of the special robe given to him by his father, tossed in a pit, and sold into slavery by his brothers. While in faithful and honorable service to his master, he was falsely accused and sent to prison. Joseph had absolutely no reason to ever find himself in the circumstances he faced.

However, in the midst of the inexplicable, he did the one thing that overcomers do: he remained faithful. He was an honest, loyal, and diligent worker for his master. Because of his attitude, he found favor in his master's eyes. He remained faithful even in prison. Because of his actions, he was trusted by the guards and given a position of authority within the prison. He was remaining faithful in a little and, whether he realized it or not, he was also allowing the Lord to shape him into the leader who would one day save Egypt and his family.

While Joseph is an example of a person who was unwittingly thrust into a wilderness experience, most people enter the wilderness through a conscious choice on their part to follow the Lord. When you make the deliberate choice to alter the course of your life based on the Lord's leading, you can become discouraged when your circumstances appear to reflect failure. Your choices and the results of those decisions make no sense to you, let alone your friends and family. From all outward appearances, you often look like a fool. The Bible clearly explains this saying, "Do not deceive yourselves. If any of you think you are wise by the standards of this age, you should become 'fools' so that you may become wise. For the wisdom of this world is foolishness in God's sight" (1 Corinthians 3:18-19a, NIV). During these times, we need to remember that God operates apart from human reasoning, and His ways are higher than ours.

In the 1800s, George Müller served as a Christian evangelist and director of the Ashley Down Orphanage in Bristol, England. As an excellent example of someone who very consciously followed the Lord's leading wherever it led him, he devoted his entire life to obeying the Lord's calling. In his own words, George Müller described his life, saying, "I have joyfully dedicated my whole life to the object of exemplifying how much may be accomplished by prayer and faith."[3]

While the Lord led George Müller to many great accomplishments over the course of his life, the most notable is establishing the Ashley Down Orphanage. He lived in England when homelessness was rampant among orphaned children from poor families. These children were seen as a blight on society and often lived and died on the streets. Their only other options were prison or workhouses, both of which were as difficult as life on the streets or even worse.

The Lord put it on George Müller's heart to help these children. After much prayer, he started taking in and educating orphan children. In the beginning, a tremendous flow of supplies poured into the orphanage,

---

[3] Muller, George. 1985. *The Autobiography of George Muller*. New Kensington, PA: Whitaker House. p. 94.

including money and basic staples. Then, the stream of supply mysteriously dwindled to a trickle. Every single daily need was met but at the eleventh hour.

In his journal, Müller describes in vivid detail the daily struggle during his wilderness. On September 5, 1838, his journal entry reads:

*Our hour of trial continues. The Lord mercifully has given enough to supply our daily necessities. But He gives **by the day** now, and almost **by the hour**, as we need it. Nothing came in yesterday. I sought the Lord again and again, both yesterday and today, and it seems that He is saying, "My hour is not yet come."*

I have faith in God. I believe that He will surely send help. Many pounds are needed within a few days, and there is not a penny in hand. This morning two pounds were given for the present needs by one of the laborers in the work.

Evening*. The Lord sent help to encourage me to continue to wait on Him and to trust in Him. As I was praying this afternoon, I felt fully assured that the Lord would send help. I praised Him before I saw the answer and asked Him to encourage our hearts, especially that He would not allow my faith to fail.*

A few minutes after I had prayed, the headmaster brought more than four pounds which had come in by several small donations.

And again, on September 8, 1838, he recounts:

God knows that I cannot provide for these children in my own strength. Therefore, He would not allow this burden to lie on me long without sending help. My fellow laborers in the ministry also trust in Him.

I would have to dismiss the children from under our scriptural instruction to their former companions if He does not help me.

He could prove wrong those who said, "In the beginning supplies might be expected while the ministry is new, but after a while, people will lose interest and stop supporting it."

If He did not provide, how could I explain the many remarkable answers to prayer which He had given to me previously which have shown me that this work is of God?

In some small measure I now understand the meaning of that word, "how long," which frequently occurs in the prayers of the Psalms. But even now, by the grace of God, my eyes are on Him only, and I believe that He will send help.[4]

We can feel and sense the urgency, angst, and desperation in Müller's journal entries. This daily struggle lasted for seven years. He could have easily given up, but he didn't. Instead, he clung to God and continued to have faith in the middle of his wilderness. Because of George Müller's faithfulness, Bristol, England, became a much better place.

During the process of appearing to be a fool in the world's eyes, God is teaching you to walk by faith and not by sight. We are assured, "Now He who has prepared us for this very thing is God, who also has given us the Spirit as a guarantee. For we walk by faith, not by sight" (2 Corinthians 5:5,7, NKJV). Those who have chosen to follow the Lord need to clearly and accurately know how to discern His voice. This requires a relationship of such intimacy that all else is stripped away. He must bring us to a place where we know His voice and trust His guidance above our own. A place

---

[4] Ibid., 96.

where we will follow His leading despite outward appearances, temporary setbacks, adverse conditions, being hemmed in on all sides, and worldly thoughts screaming at us.

We accomplish this through situations where we have only made it to the other side by the Lord's leading. The Lord must strip us down so that all we have left is Him. In this often painful yet beautiful place, in the midst of the maelstrom swirling around us, we cling to God for dear life because He is all we have. He does this in order to build us back up into the person who can successfully carry out the calling He has placed inside of us.

Transformation

Transformation includes the complete change of someone or something, usually a positive change. When God is in the process of making a life-altering change in us, He is not concerned about our comfort. Rather, He is focused on digging down to the root issues in our lives and fixing what is harming, hindering, or holding us back. The transformative process typically begins at the point in your journey when the Lord has completed the stripping process and begins rebuilding us.

After he was ruthlessly sold into slavery by his jealous brothers, Joseph was transformed from a spoiled and favorite son into a humble yet powerful man who saved his entire family and forgave his brothers. Due to a famine, Joseph's brothers were sent by their father to Egypt to purchase food for the family. Joseph had the option of treating his brothers as they had treated him but instead chose to show them compassion. He not only gave them food, he also made arrangements with Pharaoh for his family to live with him in Egypt.

However, his transformation went beyond compassion to complete forgiveness. After their father's death, Joseph's brothers were afraid that he would hold a grudge and exact revenge on them. In response to their fears, Joseph addresses his brothers saying, "'You intended to harm me, but God intended it for good to accomplish what is now being done, the saving of many lives. So then, don't be afraid. I will provide for you and your children.' And he reassured them and spoke kindly to them" (Genesis 50:20-21, NIV).

Joseph expresses a key element involved in transformation when he addresses his brothers. That element is the ability to see the Lord's hand in adversity. Instead of allowing the situation to define him and steal his hope, Joseph overcame and ultimately realized that the Lord was always in control. In fact, the Lord took what was meant to harm him and turned it into something good.

George Müller possessed the same ability to see God in all of his circumstances. Seven years into his season of hourly dependence on the Lord to provide for the orphans, he wrote this in his journal on September 1, 1838:

"The Lord in His wisdom and love has not yet sent help. Where it comes from is not my concern. But I believe God will, in due time, send help. His hour is not yet come. This is the most trying time that I have had in the ministry concerning finances. But I know that I will yet praise the Lord for His help."[5]

In this journal entry, Müller expresses two pivotal points regarding transformation. The first element is the place where one no longer demands that God do things according to our understanding or timing. At this point, we have seen God's faithfulness to the point where we no longer need to be in control. At the same time, we not only trust that help is coming but that what God will provide is better than what we would have asked Him to provide. The second pivotal point is the ability to praise the Lord in the midst of our struggles. The spiritual principal is that praise ushers in the Lord's presence and changes the atmosphere around us.

As he allowed the Lord to transform him over his lifetime, Müller cared for 10,000 orphans. He was well-known for providing an excellent education to the children under his care even to the point of being accused of raising the poor above their station in life. He also established over 100 schools that offered Christian education to over 120,000 children, many of whom were orphans.[6]

In addition, during his lifetime, Müller raised the equivalent of over $100,000,000 in today's money. How did he receive this money? Through answered prayer alone. He never asked for money but petitioned the Lord privately for everything. He gave away all of the money

---

[5] Ibid., 94.
[6] Muller, Stan. Date unknown. "George Muller: His Life and Ministry."
http://www.georgemuller.org/uploads/4/8/6/5/48652749/george_muller_seminar_stan_murrell.pdf.

he raised, using it to fund orphanages and outreach ministries.

As with every other person in history that the Lord has used greatly, George Müller's transformation came in the midst of the trials and temptations of the wilderness. His story is recorded because he allowed the circumstances around him to change him for the better rather than defeat him. George Müller described this process in his own words, saying, "It is through trials that Faith is exercised and developed more and more."

The Lord has also worked in a similar way in my own transformation. Many years ago, my husband and I recognized that the Lord was extending an invitation to us to go deeper in Him. We came to a place where the Lord asked us to take a tremendous leap of faith without any understanding. After much prayer, we decided to follow the Lord into the unknown. During this time, we were part of a small, tight-knit community of believers who walked alongside us.

Our family then faced seven of some of the most challenging years imaginable. Nothing in our lives made any sense. We continued being completely faithful to the Lord in everything He asked us to do during that time, giving our full effort to all we were asked to do. However, from outward circumstances, everything thing we did appeared to fail.

About four years into this journey, we were eating dinner at a friend's house, someone who was part of our small community of believers. At the end of dinner, as we were outside saying goodbye, our friend expressed his gratitude for the privilege of walking with us during our journey. He went on to say that he saw us as completely changed people. He told us of the strength that he saw in us and how our transformation gave him hope for the challenges he was facing in his own life.

The Lord's ultimate goal in the transformation of His people is changing our nature. We are transformed from needing to be in control to realizing that we aren't. We have peace about letting God be in control. We are growing into a place where following the Lord is more important to us than anything else. We realize that, despite everything else going on, as we let go of control, we find vast freedom in trusting and following the Lord's leading.

Redemption

The simple definition of redemption is: "the act of making something better or more acceptable." However, the word holds a much greater depth and meaning. The root word in "redemption" is "redeem." The full definition of redeem found in the Merriam-Webster Dictionary includes the following details:

transitive verb

1. a : to buy back : repurchase
   b : to get or win back
2. to free from what distresses or harms : as
   a. to free from captivity by payment of ransom
   b. to extricate from or help to overcome something detrimental
   c. to release from blame or debt : clear
   d. to free from the consequences of sin
3. to change for the better : reform
4. repair, restore

5. a. to free from a lien by payment of an amount secured thereby
   b. to remove the obligation of payment
      i. to exchange for something of value
      ii. to make good : fulfill
6. a. to atone for : expiate
   b. to offset the bad effect of
      i. to make worthwhile[7]

Redemption includes complete and utter restoration of every human condition or situation a person could ever encounter. The word "redeem" is a transitive verb which means that the action is transferred from one person or thing to another; basically, the action is done to someone or something. Simply put, redemption is an action taken by someone to benefit another. As the recipient, you have not taken any action to receive redemption. It is a gift freely given by God or by someone else.

Another element of redemption involves deliverance and rescue. God delivered Joseph from prison to become the second most powerful man in Egypt and to save his family. Joseph had an encounter with Pharaoh's cupbearer while in prison. He interpreted a dream for the man and in return, requested of him, "But when all goes well with you, remember me and show me kindness; mention me to Pharaoh and get me out of this prison. I was forcibly carried off from the land of the Hebrews, and even here I have done nothing to deserve being put in a dungeon" (Genesis 40:14-15, NIV). However, the cupbearer forgot about Joseph as soon as

---

[7] *Merriam-Webster Dictionary*. 2017. https://www.merriam-webster.com/dictionary/redeem. Accessed July 3, 2017.

he was restored to good standing with Pharaoh. Often, like Joseph, we try to redeem ourselves from unpleasant circumstances.

The Lord patiently waits until the complete fulfillment of everything He wishes to accomplish in us before He releases us into the future that He has destined for us. His restoration is then better than anything we could try to conjure for ourselves, especially when those actions are often birthed out of desperation to escape a painful or difficult circumstance. What the Lord restores, He improves upon.

When the timing was right, the Lord took Joseph from prison to a position of power and influence overnight and unexpectedly. Pharaoh was plagued with distressing dreams that no one could interpret when the cupbearer remembered his encounter with Joseph. On the cupbearer's recommendation, Joseph was brought before Pharaoh where he accurately interpreted his dreams that foretold of seven years of plenty followed by seven years of severe famine. In addition, Joseph also gave wise counsel to Pharaoh about how to practically plan for the famine to ensure Egypt's survival. Genesis recounts Joseph's redemption:

The plan seemed good to Pharaoh and to all his officials. So Pharaoh asked them, "Can we find anyone like this man, one in whom is the spirit of God?"

Then Pharaoh said to Joseph, "Since God has made all this known to you, there is no one so discerning and wise as you. You shall be in charge of my palace, and all my people are to submit to your orders. Only with respect to the throne will I be greater than you."

So Pharaoh said to Joseph, "I hereby put you in charge of the whole land of Egypt." Then Pharaoh took his signet ring from his finger and put it on Joseph's finger. He dressed him in robes of fine linen and put a gold chain around his neck. He had him ride in a chariot as his second-in-command, and people shouted before him, "Make way!" Thus he put him in charge of the whole land of Egypt.

Then Pharaoh said to Joseph, "I am Pharaoh, but without your word no one will lift hand or foot in all Egypt" (Genesis. 41:37-44, NIV).

The Lord's redemption often comes swiftly and unexpectedly. In the midst of a seemingly impossible or insurmountable challenge, the situation is suddenly and miraculously solved. We have done all that we can do and are still standing in a posture of faith, but the solution comes due to no effort on our part and could only have occurred with divine intervention. We don't ever see the answer coming, but we know that it was God.

I believe the Lord does this for two purposes. First, we cannot think that our own efforts rescued us, which could ultimately lead us into being trapped by a performance mentality. Second, we will then have absolutely no doubt that God moved on our behalf because He loves us. With all of these elements put together—our actions by faith, the wilderness journey, reformation, and restoration—we emerge as a completely changed person.

It is very evident when God has changed a person. Their countenance, demeanor, and actions all reflect the clear presence of God dwelling inside them. They stand out from other people, revealing that they are set apart.

Wisdom is in their counsel. They have an inner strength and peace that is baffling to the world. Their guidance clearly comes from the Lord because of the depth of the oneness they have with Him.

If you find yourself in the midst of any of these circumstances, you are in great company as it means that you have stepped out in faith to follow the Lord and are experiencing your own epic journey. Those that the Lord has used in a mighty way lived anything but ordinary lives. Abraham, Joseph, the Apostle Paul, all the disciples, George Müller, and many others throughout history who have dared to truly follow the Lord wherever He led them all lived extraordinary lives.

The writer of Hebrews best summarizes what it truly means to follow the Lord:

Do you see what this means — all these pioneers who blazed the way, all these veterans cheering us on? It means we'd better get on with it. Strip down, start running — and never quit! No extra spiritual fat, no parasitic sins. Keep your eyes on Jesus, who both began and finished this race we're in. Study how he did it. Because he never lost sight of where he was headed — that exhilarating finish in and with God — he could put up with anything along the way: Cross, shame, whatever. And now he's there, in the place of honor, right alongside God. When you find yourselves flagging in your faith, go over that story again, item by item, that long litany of hostility he plowed through. That will shoot adrenaline into your souls! (Hebrews 12:1-3, MSG).

LESSON 3: TRUST

WHAT DOES IT MEAN TO trust the Lord? How does trusting Him look and feel? How would that trust change our lives? How would we live our lives differently as a result?

Since the Industrial Age at the turn of the nineteenth century, people have generally turned to science and reason to decipher the baffling mysteries of the ages. Rather than trusting in the Lord, we have come to rely on our own human reasoning to navigate our lives and solve our problems. God has been reduced to a 'last resort.'

We need to live from a place of trust regarding some pivotal and all-encompassing areas in our lives in order to fully grow and develop into the fullness of who the Lord has created us to be in the earth. As we begin to embrace the Lord and allow Him access into any one of these areas, a ripple affect happens in the rest of our lives in the areas that need transformation regarding trust. The Lord needs to guide us to a place in which we can trust that He will be: our provider, the defender of our reputation, and the fulfiller of His promises. As a result of trusting, we enjoy a life filled with peace, joy, thankfulness, contentment, and experiencing miracles.

Provision

In the Old Testament of the Bible, the Hebrews used many names when referring to God. Each name related to a unique aspect of God's character as well as a facet of

His relationship with His children. One of those names is Jehovah-Jireh, which means 'The Lord Will Provide.'

So often, especially in Western culture, we easily forget that the Lord provides for us. The cares and concerns of our rapid-paced, high-tech lifestyle barrage us, pervading nearly all our thoughts. For most, the daily struggle to survive financially is all encompassing and consumes the vast majority of their time, energy, and mental capacity. Most people feel that the burden of financial provision rests fully on their shoulders.

This is not a new concern. Worrying about how one's needs will be met has existed throughout history. In his book, *Walden*, Henry David Thoreau addressed this topic saying, "How vigilant we are! Determined not to live by faith if we can avoid it; all the day long on the alert, at night we unwillingly say our prayers and commit ourselves to uncertainties."[8] What will purposely draw people toward living a life of daily anxiety over the rest they could have through a life of faith for daily provision? I believe two issues hinder people from living a life of faith: fear and a lack of trust.

Fear is a gripping, powerful, and all-encompassing human emotion, which is why the enemy plays upon people's fears. He knows that if he plays upon that emotion long enough and hard enough, he can completely debilitate a person. And why do most people fear relying on the Lord for provision? While there are any number of answers, the most common include fear of: the unknown, change, and failure. However, the

---

[8] Thoreau, Henry David. 1965 and 1992. *Walden and Other Writings*. Random House. pp. 10-11.

biggest fear that hinders most people from living in faith is a secret fear that the Lord will not take care of them. This fear ties directly into the second issue, which is a lack of trust.

If you can't trust the Lord to meet even your simplest and most basic needs, how can you trust Him for truly important matters? You can't. This is why most people are willing to "commit ourselves to uncertainties" because trusting the Lord seems like an even more uncertain outcome. Why do so many people not trust the Lord? Because they feel that the Lord has failed them in the past.

Has the Lord truly failed these people or is it a misperception? As humans, we have a tendency to place expectations upon the Lord. We expect the Lord to work according to our timing, our understanding, and our wants. God clearly made a promise to all of mankind to provide for all our needs. Never in that promise did He say when or how He would fulfill His word to us. This lack of trust creeps in when people experience difficult circumstances in their lives, go to God for help, but tie their own expectations into the outcome. The Lord fulfills His promise to them, but, when it is not in the manner or timing they expected, they often do not recognize the Lord's solution or reject it outright because it did not happen the way they wanted. They equate this with the Lord failing them, and doubt, fear, and worry begin to enter their hearts. In reality, this is an issue of focus and perspective instead.

This issue and its solution are addressed as follows:

If you decide for God, living a life of God-worship, it follows that you don't fuss about what's on the table at mealtimes or whether the clothes in your closet are in fashion. There is far more to your life than the food you put in your stomach, more to your outer appearance than the clothes you hang on your body. Look at the birds, free and unfettered, not tied down to a job description, careless in the care of God. And you count far more to him than birds.

Has anyone by fussing in front of the mirror ever gotten taller by so much as an inch? All this time and money wasted on fashion — do you think it makes that much difference? Instead of looking at the fashions, walk out into the fields and look at the wildflowers. They never primp or shop, but have you ever seen color and design quite like it? The ten best-dressed men and women in the country look shabby alongside them.

If God gives such attention to the appearance of wildflowers — most of which are never even seen — don't you think he'll attend to you, take pride in you, do his best for you? What I'm trying to do here is to get you to relax, to not be so preoccupied with 'getting,' so you can respond to God's 'giving.' People who don't know God and the way he works fuss over these things, but you know both God and how he works. Steep your life in God-reality, God-initiative, God-provisions. Don't worry about missing out. You'll find that all your everyday human concerns will be met.

Give your entire attention to what God is doing right now, and don't get worked up about what may or may not happen tomorrow. God will help you deal with whatever hard things come up when the time comes
(Matthew 6:25-34, MSG).

Many examples of God's provision have occurred throughout history that are still relevant today. Elijah was miraculously fed twice by the Lord. After Elijah spoke to Ahab and foretold a drought that would come upon the land, the Lord spoke to him, saying, "'Leave here, turn eastward and hide in the Kerith Ravine, east of the Jordan. You will drink from the brook, and I have directed the ravens to supply you with food there.' So he did what the LORD had told him. He went to the Kerith Ravine, east of the Jordan, and stayed there. The ravens brought him bread and meat in the morning and bread and meat in the evening, and he drank from the brook" (1 Kings 17:3-6, NIV).

During the drought, the brook dried up, and the Lord sent Elijah new provision by sending him to Zarapheth where a widow fed him. Elijah encountered the destitute widow at the town gate, gathering up firewood to make a loaf of bread with the last of her flour. She was so poor and in such great need that she was sure this was her and her son's last meal. But the Lord moved and provided for her family and Elijah:

"Elijah said to her, 'Don't be afraid. Go home and do as you have said. But first make a small loaf of bread for me from what you have and bring it to me, and then make something for yourself and your son. For this is what the LORD, the God of Israel, says: 'The jar of flour will not be used up and the jug of oil will not run dry until the day the LORD sends rain on the land.'"

She went away and did as Elijah had told her. So there was food every day for Elijah and for the woman and her family. For the jar of flour was not used up and the jug of oil did not run dry, in keeping with the word of the LORD spoken by Elijah" (1 Kings 17:13-16, NIV).

It's no surprise that the next example of supernatural provision from the Lord is set in the wilderness. While this example comes from the Israelites who were physically in the wilderness, most people encounter

God's provision during difficult or challenging times in life that we often refer to as a wilderness season. The Lord led the Israelites out of Egypt into the desert. When their food was running low, the people began to complain and grumble about their circumstances. God heard their grumbling and responded as follows:

"The LORD said to Moses, "I have heard the grumbling of the Israelites. Tell them, 'At twilight you will eat meat, and in the morning you will be filled with bread. Then you will know that I am the LORD your God.'"

That evening quail came and covered the camp, and in the morning there was a layer of dew around the camp. When the dew was gone, thin flakes like frost on the ground appeared on the desert floor" (Exodus 16:11-14, NIV).

During a time of hardship and desperation, we can easily be fearful. Thankfully, the Lord never responds to us based on our lack of faith. He always responds to us out of love and mercy.

In both examples, God performed miracles to feed Elijah and the Israelites. When the Lord provides for us, He often goes out of His way to make sure that we know that He was the one who supplied our need. An unexpected check for exactly the amount of money we need on the very day a bill is due shows God at work. A surprise gift card given anonymously. The person in line at the grocery store paying for our groceries. Being flat broke, needing to buy milk for a young child, feeling prompted to put a hand in our pocket, and finding $20 that wasn't there before. God can work in many ways to meet our needs using people, circumstances, or miracles.

He operates in this manner to prove His faithfulness to us. He knows that we are human, and He knows our weaknesses. The Lord is keenly aware that, without occasional acts that are glaringly obvious, as humans, we will forget that He is our provider. Without these reinforcements, we have the potential to fall back into fear and doubt. Or, out of fear or vast success, we will begin to view our work and efforts as provision. The key is to stay rooted in a place of trust where it is easier to recognize that the Lord daily meets our needs. As stated by George Müller, "Be assured, if you walk with Him and look to Him, and expect help from Him, He will never fail you."[9]

But, how, exactly does this look in our everyday lives? In the wake of the financial downturn of 2008, my husband, who was our family's sole source of income, lost his job. In the following years, the only employment that either of us could find was contract work. Sometimes, we had intervals between jobs and had to live off savings.

In 2010, we thought we were done with the worst of it and that we were on the road to recovery. My husband finally had a permanent, full-time position and had been there for seven months. And then, to our complete surprise, the Lord asked us to take a huge leap of faith. Quite clearly, He asked my husband to leave that seemingly secure job and for both of us to take on contract work at a huge pay cut in a completely new field of work. To the complete and utter astonishment and bewilderment of practically everyone who knew us, we

---

[9] *George Muller.* 2017. "George Muller Quotes." Last modified September 2, 2017. http://www.georgemuller.org/quotes.

did what the Lord asked. Over the next three and a half years, we went through what remained of our savings.

The bottom finally fell out for us in in the Fall of 2013. My husband and I were both contractors working for the same company. We were both unexpectedly let go on the same day. As contractors, we wouldn't receive unemployment benefits. We had enough money in our account to pay for one month's worth of bills. However, we were unemployed for five months.

And, so, we began a lifestyle completely and utterly dependent on the Lord's provision. Just like Müller, we did not advertise our needs to anyone. Together, we fervently took all our daily needs to the Lord in prayer.

A month later, we found ourselves with a stack of bills, our mortgage due, and no way to pay for any of them. I think the lowest point for me was when our bank account showed $1.87, we were running out of food, and my daughter opened the refrigerator and innocently asked me, "Mom, when are you going to go shopping? There's not a lot of food." It was all I could do to choke back my tears and give a calm answer that wouldn't frighten her.

Little did I know that help was to arrive very soon. Two days later, our house church group was holding its weekly gathering. It was nice to be out of our house, away from our current situation, and among caring, loving friends. At the end of the evening, I had two people, completely independent of each other, pull me aside and tell me that the Lord had put it on their hearts that we needed help. I was handed an envelope and a folded bill. When I looked at what we were given, it was enough money to pay all our bills, including our mortgage, with enough left over to buy groceries. I burst into tears. I was completely surprised and, at the same time, extremely grateful and overwhelmed by their generosity to obey the Lord's prompting.

Over the course of the next four months, this was our typical life. We had to live day by day, holding fast to the Lord, trusting Him to be faithful and provide. We finally got to the point where when we saw that we were running out of funds, my husband and I would pray together and ask the Lord for the specific amount of money we needed for the bills that were due. And, without fail, every single time we prayed, the Lord supplied more than double the amount for which we had asked. A family member paid our mortgage for two months, unexpected Christmas gifts arrived for our children, and checks and gift cards showed up in the mail.

The most poignant example happened when we were a couple of days away from missing our mortgage. My husband and I prayed for the amount of our mortgage. On the exact day that we needed it, a check for twice that amount showed up in our mailbox. When we looked at the envelope, the postmark showed seven days earlier. The Lord knew the need we had before we ever asked for help and had prompted someone to send it to us a week earlier. The provision we needed was already on its way to us before we even asked the Lord for help. And, once again, the Lord provided double what we had asked for.

While we have to rely solely upon the Lord at times like these, in most instances, we have to work in tandem with Him. We need to listen to His promptings, follow His direction and leading, and trust that He will supply exactly what we need when we need it. We have to do our part and believe that the Lord will supernaturally accomplish the things in our lives that we cannot do.

The Lord gives us talents, gifts, and passions for certain things, yet, from a young age, we are told to shove down what we enjoy and are naturally good at in pursuit of a comfortable, safe, well-paying job. We repress our God-given talents, those that He wants us to use, while living miserably, trying to scratch out an existence. Henry David Thoreau described this bleak existence, saying, "The mass of men lead lives of quiet desperation. What is called resignation is confirmed desperation."[10]

We have the notion of our life's work, or how we work to make a living, backwards. We should be pursuing a vocation that we are good at and what we are naturally passionate about. Why else would God have given us those talents and abilities? Each one of His children is a unique creation and a gift to this world. Each child of God is innately endowed with personally tailored spiritual gifts and abilities that are meant to be used to change our world for the better. What sense would it make for the Lord to give us a natural inclination toward certain gifts and then not provide for us when we used those gifts as He intended? The money and provision will flow to us as a result of stepping out in faith and trusting Him to be faithful.

Imagine a world in which all of God's children used their talents in pursuit of advancing His kingdom in the

---

[10] Thoreau, Henry David. 1965 and 1992. *Walden and Other Writings*. Random House. p. 8.

earth. Imagine the things that could be accomplished. Imagine the things that could be eradicated. Imagine the life we would experience in that world.

Reputation

Many people struggle a great deal with their reputation. We generally desire to be perceived as good, honest, decent people. We are also inherently ingrained with a desire to fit in and be accepted by those close to us.

The average person wants to live an unassuming life where they blend in with everyone else. However, as God's children, we are not average nor are we created to fit in. We are made to stand out and shine. As it says in Matthew 5:14-16, "You are the light of the world. A town built on a hill cannot be hidden. Neither do people light a lamp and put it under a bowl. Instead they put it on its stand, and it gives light to everyone in the house. In the same way, let your light shine before others, that they may see your good deeds and glorify your Father in heaven" (NIV).

We are going to be called to tasks the average person would never dare dream as possible. We will be asked to carry out God's work according to His wisdom, which is utterly baffling to man. If the common person does not understand God's ways, they will surely be confused by your actions as you follow His leading.

People fear what they do not understand or cannot control. When our beliefs and subsequent actions challenge the comfort of those around us or confront them with their own disbelief and apathy, we will encounter resistance. The change in our nature and relationship with the Lord will make them uncomfortable. They like the old person who is more like them.

Most often, it is those closest to us who will not understand us. We might commonly lose friends, be misunderstood, or even maligned. Jesus spoke about this, saying, "'A prophet is not without honor except in his own town, among his relatives and in his own home.'" He could not do any miracles there, except lay his hands on a few sick people and heal them. He was amazed at their lack of faith" (Mark 6:4-6a, NIV).

Out of sincere love or concern, family and friends might try to correct us or bring us back into line with their understanding. Their intentions will sincerely be honorable and from a place of concern for our well-being. We might also find ourselves at a crossroads where, for no apparent reason, we lose or drift apart from friends.

We might find this challenging and emotionally difficult the first time this happens. However, this is a natural and needed progression of our spiritual journey. We have changed paths and need to be aligned with friends on the same journey with the Lord. Having experienced this multiple times now, when I notice a distance appearing within a friendship, I go directly to the Lord. He might place it on my heart to let the friendship go at this time. I then pray God's best over their life and move on. I know that God has good plans for both our lives. I also trust that He will bring new people into both our lives that are the best for each of us at this particular stage of our spiritual journey.

This is why God called Abram out into the desert away from his family. The Lord told Abram, "'Go from your country, your people and your father's household to the land I will show you'" (Genesis 12:1, NIV). Abram's family were pagans and idolaters. He had to leave his family in order to grow in the Lord and change into Abraham. He had to leave well-meaning friends and family who would have sought to keep him as Abram. We might lose friends or our reputation along the way. But ultimately, it is not important what other people think about us. If our good name or reputation are damaged, the Lord is the one who will restore us. King David reminded himself of this truth, saying, "The righteous person may have many troubles, but the Lord delivers him from them all" (Psalms 34:19, NIV). Like Abraham, we are asked to trust the Lord in every area of our lives and follow Him through the unknown and into the life that He has destined for us.

Fulfill His Promises

Abram believed the Lord and was considered righteous. This encounter between God and Abram is recorded in Genesis as, "And Abram believed the LORD, and the LORD counted him as righteous because of his faith" (Genesis 15:6, NLT). It took twenty-five years for Abraham to see the fulfillment of the Lord's promise of a son. However, Abraham continued in faith the whole time.

Many years later, the Lord asked Abraham to sacrifice his long-awaited, promised son, Isaac. Abraham journeyed with his son and prepared to sacrifice him, trusting that the Lord would provide an alternative sacrifice. He also believed that if he sacrificed Isaac, the Lord could raise the boy from the dead. In fact, the Lord had provided an alternative sacrifice, and at the last moment, showed Abraham a ram caught in a thicket.

Timing is one of the biggest stumbling blocks for people in the area of trusting God to fulfill His promises. The Lord is focused on shaping and sculpting us so that we can properly handle the blessings He gives us. That process often takes a long time. We tend to be impatient and in a hurry. The longer it takes to receive our promise, the more likely we are to begin to waver in faith and to doubt. Thankfully, examples like Abraham remind us of God's faithfulness. If you have been waiting for a long time to see a promise come to pass, you are in good company. The Lord made Abraham wait a very long time!

Just like Abraham, the Lord tests us to see if we still trust Him after receiving our reward. Is He still the most important thing in our lives? Do we love Him more than what He has given us? These tests are just as important to us as they are to God. If we do not keep God as the center of our lives, trusting only in Him, the very things that the Lord gives us as blessings could inadvertently become detrimental to us.

Twenty-five years ago, when I was a senior in high school, the Lord gave me two vivid and detailed prophetic dreams one night. In the first dream, I was at an elementary school, talking to a woman who I couldn't see because the sun was behind her and the glare was hurting my eyes. I was explaining to her that I had met the man of my dreams, that we planned to be married, and that I was moving out of state to join him. In the middle of our conversation, the last bell of the day rang, announcing dismissal, and the halls flooded with children as we finished talking.

The second dream started immediately afterwards. In that dream, I was inside a beautiful, peaceful, and comfortable home with my children. I can't begin to describe the depth of warmth and love flowing between me and my children. We heard something outside and went through a set of French doors onto a balcony on the second story of the house.

Once we were in the light, I could clearly see my children. My oldest child was a girl, and my youngest was a boy. Both children had blond hair and sky-blue eyes.

We heard my husband arriving home from work. As he got out of the car, the kids and I ran down the stairs to meet him. We reached the front door and ran outside to my husband. The kids beat me to him and were already hugging him, when I wrapped my arms around everyone and gave my husband a kiss.

As we turned to go back inside, I caught a glimpse of the house. It was a gorgeous and immense traditional two-story home in light blue with white shutters and a white extended patio on columns that was accessible through French doors on the second story. In the entryway, the house had beautiful wainscoting along the wall next to the stairs. A small white picket fence lined the edge of the property, setting off a large and lush green lawn, and a bricked walkway lead up to the front door. It was, in every sense, a "dream house."

Exactly five years later to the month, I was a senior in college just a few weeks away from graduating, and I was madly in love (and still am) with the man who is now my husband. Somehow, the Lord coordinated circumstances so that I worked in an after-school daycare program at the elementary school that my husband attended as a child. At the time, I was making plans to move halfway across the country to join my then boyfriend whose job had transferred him a few months earlier. I was standing in the hallway of the school right before my shift, and I ran into a co-worker. She had heard I was moving and asked me about my plans. I was trying to talk to her, but it was difficult because of the glare behind her. When the bell rang and students started pouring out around us, I finally remembered my dream. The encounter happened exactly as it had in my dream.

Fast forward another five years, and we had been married a few years and started having children. Two to be exact, a girl followed by a boy. Both our children have light blond hair and sky-blue eyes, just like in my dream. The odds of one, yet alone both my children, having blue eyes is infinitesimal. My husband is half Italian with dark brown, almost black hair, and brown eyes. I, too, have brown hair and brown eyes.

Everything the Lord showed me in both dreams from more than two decades ago has come true except for one thing. The relocation, the marriage, two beautiful children, and a home filled with love have manifested. The only thing we are still waiting for is the "dream house." Now, don't get me wrong, we aren't just passively waiting, expecting it to fall from the sky; we are actively pursuing the Lord and doing whatever He puts on our hearts to do as our part to help bring this to pass. I have no doubt that the "dream house" is part of our future. My husband and I continue to move forward in faith, believing that one day, the house will be part of our reality, and then the promise will be complete.

The Lord has even been gracious enough to give us confirmation from more than one source that the "dream house" is a reality for our future. About ten years ago, our family attended a ministry event. A man we had never met before stood up and said he had a word for our family. He said that he saw the mantle of ministry over us. He also said that he saw a big, beautiful house in our future. This man ended by saying that we would minister and help broken and hurting people in our house and that we would be just as blessed as those that we helped.

The last confirmation came in the form of a dream the Lord gave my husband. While the Lord gave me a detailed view of the outside of the house, He showed my husband details of the inside. The Lord showed my husband the intricate wainscoting and then a study across from the stairs. The entrance to the study was a beautiful set of French doors. My husband described the inside of the study with intricate millwork throughout, including custom-built shelves and bookcases in a rich mahogany hue. He said that in the dream, he was sitting down to work on a computer with a screen that swiveled. At the time of the dream, this type of computer had not been developed yet. His dream ended with this feeling of complete and utter peace, contentment, and well-being in the house.

Just like Abraham, we have been waiting more than twenty-five years now, but like him, my husband and I will continue to trust the Lord. And, just like anyone else the Lord makes a promise to, He will continue to send affirmation and confirmation to me and to you. For example, He sent angels disguised as travelers to Abraham to announce the coming of his promised child through his wife, Sarah. For my family, encouragement and reassurance has come in the form of dreams, words from perfect strangers, and many other means.

Our challenge is to continue in faith and not lose heart during the waiting as we recognize encouragement from the Lord along the way. The Lord's heart is always to do good to us, as He says in Jeremiah 29:11, "'For I know the plans I have for you,' declares the LORD, 'plans to prosper you and not to harm you, plans to give you hope and a future'"(NIV). Only the Lord truly understands the timing of what He intends for us. The passage of time does not diminish the validity of the promise. It just makes it that much sweeter and more meaningful when we receive what the Lord always intended for us.

Benefits of Trusting the Lord

One of the most immediate and powerful benefits of trusting the Lord is His peace. This peace is described in Philippians as, "Then you will experience God's peace, which exceeds anything we can understand. His peace will guard your hearts and minds as you live in Christ Jesus" (Philippians 4:7, NLT). The Lord's peace is all-encompassing and enriches every area of our lives. This peace always sustains us and helps us live with less stress, knowing that He is faithful because the Lord has always come through for us.

Trust allows us to witness miracles. Through the eyes of faith, we see the impossible occur. When I was five years old, my mom had a stroke, caused by a condition she was born with, a malformation between the arteries and veins inside her brain. Within the medical community, this condition is called an Arteriovenous Malformation or AVM.

My mom was born in 1949, well before many of the technological breakthroughs that have advanced modern medicine. Her condition wasn't properly diagnosed until 1976, when CT Scan machines were first being installed. In fact, part of the technology used to help save my mom's life wasn't invented until shortly before her stroke. Due to the location of the lemon-sized blood clot deep inside her brain, the doctors were afraid to do surgery, fearing that it would cause a stroke. Instead, they decided to wait and perform surgery when it burst. To be honest, most of the medical staff associated with my mom's case thought that she was a lost cause and that death was inevitable.

On Thanksgiving Day of 1979, a rupture caused bleeding inside my mom's brain. She underwent two groundbreaking surgeries using new techniques and medical equipment to correct the bleeding. Given the location of the AVM and the newness of these procedures, no prognosis was really given regarding her outcome. The surgeries on my mom were considered more exploratory or experimental in nature because no one thought she would survive them. The medical community saw this as an opportunity to learn more about the brain and develop techniques that would help people in the future.

My mom survived the surgeries but was left paralyzed on her left side. Her doctors considered this the best possible outcome. They told my dad that she would be paralyzed for the rest of her life and that he needed to start preparing her for her new reality. My mom staunchly believed that she would have a complete and full recovery, including the use of her left side. She never yielded or wavered in her belief that the Lord would completely restore her. My dad didn't have the heart to take away that hope from her and planned to wait until they were home to ease her into her new life.

Again, God moved on her behalf! Feeling began to return to the left side of her body. One day, while my dad was with her in her hospital room, she surprised him by wiggling a finger on her left hand. However, her recovery was far from complete. With intense and grueling physical therapy, to the amazement of her doctors, she made a full recovery—with no medical explanation from her doctors!

She is able to walk, drive, and even returned to her career as a nurse. She has amazed and surprised her doctors at every turn. Her doctors only gave her a post-surgery life expectancy of five years, which she never believed. More than thirty-five years have now passed since her stroke. Her unyielding faith in the Lord created numerous miracles. I was fortunate to witness from a very young age the power of trust and faith and to see first-hand that nothing is impossible with the Lord.

Another attribute of trust is joy. A simple definition of joy is a feeling of great happiness. We experience happiness because we know much we are cared for and how deeply we are loved. The level of love and care the Lord has for His children is clearly expressed in Matthew 10:29-31, "Are not two sparrows sold for a penny? Yet not one of them will fall to the ground outside your Father's care. And even the very hairs of your head are all numbered. So don't be afraid; you are worth more than many sparrows" (NIV).

If the Lord has taken such a detailed account of our being that He is aware of the exact number of hairs on our heads, what part of us or our lives does He not care about? He is acutely aware of every aspect of our lives and is fully engaged in taking care of us. This is a cause for joy and rest. As Paul wrote, "May the God of hope fill you with all joy and peace as you trust in him, so that you may overflow with hope by the power of the Holy Spirit" (Romans 15:13, NIV). This posture of hope-filled rest ties into the next attribute of trusting the Lord, which is thankfulness.

Being thankful is a conscious decision to be grateful for what the Lord gives us and how He helps us every day. Even a single thought of gratitude toward the Lord for His help begins to change our hearts. It also changes our thoughts and thought patterns until, over time, our tendency is to be happy and satisfied with our lives. Being thankful becomes a natural and regular expression. Thankfulness begets more thankfulness and opens up the flow of giving into our lives. We begin to see God working on our behalf in our daily life. At this point, we are thankful for the little things and every aspect of our lives, including the challenges that we sometimes face. And this ultimately leads us to contentment.

When we live in a state of contentment, we see all the attributes of trust working together: peace, miracles, joy, and thankfulness. We no longer need to be in control.

We are not worried about outcomes or how the Lord goes about accomplishing things in our lives. The timing of God's promises is unimportant. We live each day one day at a time, knowing that our future is secure in the Lord's hands.

A life surrendered to God is in itself a dichotomy. God's ways are counterintuitive and, at times, seemingly contradictory. Our yielding and suppleness to Him is what creates our strength. We only become immovable and immutable forces in His Kingdom from a stance of rest and trust in the Lord.

LESSON 4: COMMUNICATE

WHAT DOES IT MEAN TO talk to God? How does that look or feel? How will I recognize when the Lord is speaking to me? These are just a few of the questions people face when they consciously try to communicate with the Lord for the first time.

In our noisy and distracting world, many things vie for our attention or scream at us from inside our own heads. Many people have been taught that God no longer communicates directly with His people. Alternatively, they might be taught that He only speaks in one manner—through the Bible. At first, they might struggle to discover and recognize the Lord's voice in the midst of everything else.

Whether or not we realize it, the Lord has been speaking to us our entire lives. In Job 33:14, it says, "For God speaks again and again, though people do not recognize it"(NLT). It is a matter of recognizing the many ways in which the Lord communicates. His intentions and means of expressing Himself are personally tailored to us.

I believe people often miss the numerous ways the Lord speaks because His methods are so subtle. He is always right beside us so He doesn't need to speak loudly. He is also a gentleman, so He does not force Himself on us. Because of how the Lord speaks to us and because He is constantly with us, most people mistake His overtures as chance or coincidence.

Over the course of my life, I have become attuned to ways the Lord speaks. The initial challenge is in recognizing how He interacts with us individually. Thankfully, as soon as you discern any type of communication, hearing Him becomes easier with each interaction. The main methods of communication the Lord uses include: speaking directly, speaking through others, speaking through circumstances, and alternative means of communication.

Speaking Directly

Examples of how the Lord speaks to us directly include:

- Impressions on our heart
- Gentle but consistent reminders
- Dreams
- Visions
- On rare occasions, hearing His voice

The prophet Samuel provides one example of someone the Lord spoke to directly. However, he needed help at first recognizing His voice. Samuel was the son of Hannah, a woman who had been barren for many years. She went to the temple to pray for a child; in return for God granting her prayer, she offered to give that child back to the Lord to serve Him. God granted her prayer, and as soon as Samuel was weened, she took him to the temple to be raised by Eli, the priest.

When he was a young boy, the Lord spoke to Samuel for the first time. That encounter with the Lord is recorded in 1 Samuel 3:3b-10 (NIV):

Samuel was lying down in the house of the LORD, where the ark of God was. Then the LORD called Samuel.

Samuel answered, "Here I am." And he ran to Eli and said, "Here I am; you called me."

But Eli said, "I did not call; go back and lie down." So he went and lay down.

Again the LORD called, "Samuel!" And Samuel got up and went to Eli and said, "Here I am; you called me."

"My son," Eli said, "I did not call; go back and lie down."

Now Samuel did not yet know the LORD: The word of the LORD had not yet been revealed to him.

A third time the LORD called, "Samuel!" And Samuel got up and went to Eli and said, "Here I am; you called me."

Then Eli realized that the LORD was calling the boy. So Eli told Samuel, "Go and lie down, and if he calls you, say, 'Speak, LORD, for your servant is listening.'" So Samuel went and lay down in his place.

The LORD came and stood there, calling as at the other times, "Samuel! Samuel!"

Then Samuel said, "Speak, for your servant is listening."

As recorded in history, Samuel went on to become one of the major prophets in the Old Testament. Even so, he didn't recognize the Lord's voice at first. The Lord will either confirm that He is the one speaking or, as with Samuel, He will use a more seasoned person to help you recognize the Lord's voice.

Furthermore, this exchange took place at night right as Samuel was falling asleep. The Lord commonly speaks to us at dusk or dawn, which are the intervals between being asleep and awake. Pay special attention to feelings, impressions, or thoughts you have at these times; the Lord might be communicating with you.

Often, what people consider "sixth sense" or "intuition" is really the Lord speaking to us. A few years ago, the Lord put a former high school friend on my husband's heart. He hadn't seen or talked to this friend in years. Over the course of several months, my husband mentioned that this man was in his thoughts and that he needed to give him a call. My husband had every good intention of calling his friend, but life always got in the way, and he never ended up speaking to him.

As it turned out, his friend was in an extremely dark place, and sadly, the man ended up taking his own life. My husband was devastated by his friend's death because he realized the Lord had been prompting him to call his friend who was in need of help. After this experience, he vowed that if the Lord ever put anyone on his heart again, he would reach out to them because the Lord had a specific purpose in bringing them to mind.

Speaking Through Other People

Examples of how the Lord speaks to us through others include:

- "Divine appointments"
- People directly speaking to us
    - Prophetic words
    - Impressions or things on their heart they feel they need to share

I use the term "divine appointments" for interactions I have with other people that I have not planned but that are clearly orchestrated by the Lord. A few months ago, I was shopping for groceries. I turned down the spice aisle. At the end of the aisle was a woman. She asked me a question about a product she was interested in purchasing. As we started talking, I felt a connection with her even though we had never met before. We ended up talking for over an hour and exchanging contact information.

We tried to get together shortly thereafter, but it just didn't work out. Three months went by without any communication between us, and, at that point, I assumed she wouldn't remember me. Then, out of the blue, I received a text from her inviting me to coffee. We met and had a wonderful time. To the amazement of both of us, the Lord gave her a prophetic word for me and my family.

What she didn't know was how timely her words were and how much I needed to hear what she shared from the Lord's heart. Everything she spoke about touched on an area where I had been struggling or on things that my husband and I had been discussing not more than a couple of days earlier. The thing she shared that resonated the most with me related to a window of time that started in January 2017.

She spoke of a pregnancy-like gestational period of nine months. The Lord was going to be imparting some things to us that would be pivotal for our calling, and He was asking us to come up higher in Him during this time. Just like a baby is protected in its mother's womb, she shared that we had absolutely nothing to fear and that the Lord would be watching out for us and taking care of us. She said that the Lord was going to be making changes in us that would benefit us and impact our extended family.

She mentioned a double-blessing, double-portion over me and my husband individually and collectively as a couple. The last impression she shared was that we couldn't even begin to imagine what He was about to do for us and that it was better than anything we could have ever dreamed. In the end, we will be laughing at the sheer goodness of what the Lord has done and that our hard times or dark days are over.

Just two days before we met for coffee, my husband and I had a similar discussion. It was near the end of the year, and I remembered that on January 1, it would be exactly seven years since the Lord asked us to take a massive leap of faith and follow Him out into the unknown. This leap of faith that I discussed earlier plunged us into some of the hardest and darkest days of our married life. Seven is a number denoting completion and miracles. I commented to my husband that we were coming upon a time of completion for our current season. My husband became excited because the Lord had impressed upon him that we had a breakthrough coming in October of the following year. He then connected that there are nine months between January and October, just like in a human pregnancy.

My new friend spoke about a couple of other things that she could not have known about in the natural. The first thing was that eleven years ago, two women that we met while on vacation prophesied that we would be moving back to our hometown. These women prophesied that the people going back would not be the same people who had left. They also said that our family and friends were not going to like the changes in us, but the Lord was going to use the changes to positively affect those around us. And lastly, my friend had no idea that the morning we met for coffee, the Lord woke me up by singing repeatedly, "The dark days are over now; your dark days are over."

I have no doubt in my mind that this was a divine appointment. It was clear that the Lord was guiding our conversation. She listed several specific things pertaining to my life—past, present, and future—that she could not have known on her own. When all of these elements come together, the Lord is clearly going out of His way to bring confirmation, clarity, and peace to you concerning your life or your current circumstances.

Speaking Through Circumstances

One example of how the Lord speaks to us through circumstances:

- Seeing meaning or correlations between things happening in our life or those around us

Object Lessons

I use the term "object lessons" for experiences in life that teach me a spiritual as well as a temporal lesson. I recently had an experience over a two-day period where the Lord was really trying to impress upon me the importance of trusting in His timing. It started innocently enough at a gas station. I was running late to my first meeting with this organization, so I needed to arrive on time. Of course, the gas light was on in my car, so I would have to stop for gas on my way. I swiped my card as soon as I pulled up to the pump at the gas station. I stood there for what seemed like an eternity, watching the screen beep at me, "Please Wait, Authorizing."

When my patience ran out, I went in to the attendant who informed me that the transaction had just cleared at the pump and that I could now complete my purchase. I went back to the pump. Sure enough, the screen was asking me for input. When I entered the needed information, the screen came back, "Please See Attendant." Back I went to the attendant, who was quite confused to see me again so quickly. After two back-and-forth trips, I could finally start fueling my car.

My other experience with patience and timing occurred the very next day and involved an online purchase. I ordered an item online at 35 percent off a couple weeks before and had the item shipped to the store. Due to an unexpected glitch, I never received an email confirming that my item had arrived at the store. I was surprised that my item hadn't come in yet, so I went to the store. The store attendant couldn't find my item or any record of my purchase, and I had left my receipt printout at home. I was told to call the store as soon as I had the order information, and they would see what they could do to help me.

I went home and found the information the store clerk needed. When I called the store with my order number, I was informed that because I hadn't picked the item up on time, the sale had been cancelled. However, the person I spoke to was willing to check and see if it was still in the store. Thankfully, this attendant was able to find my order; she placed it on hold for me to come back and purchase. When I went back to the store, my item had been marked on clearance, and I ended up purchasing it at 70 percent off. What an incredible surprise and blessing!

Interestingly, both experiences involved delays and a need for patience. However, there were slight differences. At the gas station, my impatience caused an unnecessary delay. With the online purchase, through no fault of my own, an unexpected delay yielded an equally unexpected blessing. The Lord will do things in my life according to His own timing. I need to be patient and expect that, at some point, a blessing will come as a result of my patience.

Alternative Means of Communication

Although this list is by no means exhaustive, examples of how the Lord speaks to us through alternative means of communication include:

- Music/Songs
- Media
  - Social media
  - Movies
  - TV
- Articles of clothing, such as shirts with words on them
- Printed materials
  - Bible
  - Books
  - Magazines
  - Pamphlets
  - Flyers
  - Billboards
  - Fortune cookies
- Art
  - Paintings
  - Pictures
  - Other mediums of art
- Secular and Non-Christian Means

The list of alternative ways the Lord uses to speak to us is as large and varied as each individual. I commonly encounter the Lord speaking to me through these means that might not always be obvious or expected.

I might see or hear multiple things from the Lord during the course of my day. A couple of years ago, my husband and I enjoyed a rare night out. Finances were tight, but we felt strongly led by the Lord to make reservations at a fairly expensive restaurant that we'd never eaten at before.

The restaurant, Harvest Seasonal Kitchen, is located in the heart of a quaint and romantic historic downtown square. It boasts a farm-to-table concept with an interior design of upscale, rustic farm ambiance with soft ethereal lighting. The hostess led us to table twenty-two, a cozy, two-person mahogany-colored table nestled deep in the heart of the restaurant.

My eyes were immediately drawn to the regal-looking, high-backed chairs covered in soft blue velour. As I sat down, I glanced at the painting above our seating area, a farm-themed, charcoal drawing of a fruit basket, titled "Fruit of Labors." We feasted on the most scrumptious locally sourced produce, meats, and wines. Of course, since this was a rare splurge, we overindulged and extended our dinner into dessert and coffee.

Deliriously over-stuffed, we decided to stroll around the downtown square after dinner. Most of the buildings on the square were built in the late 1800s to early 1900s. As we were turning the first corner of our walk, something above me caught my glance—the fading name "Hope & Sons" on an old brick building.

We next walked by a waitress on her break sitting by the back door of the restaurant where she worked; her t-shirt graphic said "There's Lovin' over There." As we passed her, a co-worker of hers came out and struck up a conversation. His shirt had a large, edgy eagle graphic in the center.

We continued walking until our stomachs were comfortable enough to return to our car and ended our night with a drive through the country. As we neared our car, I glimpsed the silhouette of a near-to-term pregnant woman in the distance. We reached our car and began driving out of the square, passing a beautiful black Range Rover.

All of these details might seem random, haphazard, or even insignificant to the average person, but the Lord orchestrated our entire evening and was speaking to me throughout the course of our date night. For several years, our family had been in a very challenging wilderness season that seemed to have no end in sight. Recently, the Lord has been communicating to us that we are transitioning into a better season. It didn't strike me until we pulled up in front of the restaurant. I then saw the sleek modern "Harvest" sign, and the Lord reminded me that we are moving into a time of harvest in our own lives.

The small downtown square was buzzing with people, and we were running late, so my husband dropped me off to check in while he found a parking spot. The hostess looked up our reservation, turned to her assistant, and said, "They'll be dining at table twenty-two." My heart immediately leapt for joy because the spiritual significance of the number two is a double-blessing; twenty-two conveyed a double-double blessing to me. The Lord was communicating the same theme again through a slightly different means.

While I was sitting at our table waiting for my husband to join me, my attention was constantly drawn to the beautiful vacant blue chair across from me. As I stared, a gentle thought came to my mind that blue is the color of royalty, and we are his children, which makes us royal. My husband joined me, and we began our date.

During dinner, my eyes kept being drawn to the painting at our table. Finally, things connected when I read the title, "Fruit of Labor." Amidst many years of trying difficulties, my husband and I have faithfully sown into the lives of anyone the Lord has put on our hearts without ever seeing any change in our own circumstances. I nearly cried in the restaurant as I felt the Lord impress upon me that we were going to see the fruits of our labors and reap the benefits of the seeds that we had sown. The fancy restaurant and change of scene as well as the ways the Lord directed our dinner all pointed toward the themes He has been speaking to us recently of a coming harvest and transition into a time of prosperity.

As we walked after dinner, the Lord continued to speak to and encourage me. He conveyed a message of hope to me through the name "Hope & Sons" on the historic building. The t-shirt the waitress wore reminded me of the Lord's love and that there is even more of His love waiting for us "over there" in the new place He has prepared for us.

I have always liked eagles and hawks with their majestic and sweeping movements of flight, soaring high above the earth. For some reason, I always feel better when I see hawks and am filled with the thought that something good is about to happen. The co-worker's t-shirt, depicting an eagle in flight, reinforced the message of hope the Lord had given me mere seconds earlier.

We then turned to go back to our car, and I glimpsed the pregnant woman who was nearly full term. Seeing her reminded me of the Lord's recent messages that we are entering a new season and the impression that He has given us recently that He is birthing something new in us. It also gave me hope that the advanced stage of her pregnancy might mean that we are closer than we know to the new thing the Lord has for us.

Range Rovers are my dream car, and my favorite color for them is black. Whether I ever own one or not, they are beautiful, and just looking at one makes me smile. Everything that is important to us is also important to the Lord. Seeing that Range Rover at the end of our evening was the culmination of everything the Lord had been speaking to me all night—hold onto hope because I am transitioning you to a new place that is wonderful. The examples shown throughout the course of our evening illustrate how the Lord uses many ways to communicate with us.

Another way, albeit somewhat controversial, the Lord speaks with us is one that many people don't even consider. The Lord can use anything or anyone to communicate with us, which means He also uses secular culture and non-Christians. Because everything and everyone on earth is made by God, He can use anything as His mouthpiece; often, non-believers don't even realize the Lord is speaking through them or using them as His instrument.

The Lord commonly speaks to me through music. Some of my more traditional Christian friends might be very surprised to know that the Lord has used songs by rap artists, such as Eminem and Ace Hood, to encourage me. Eminem's songs "Not Afraid" and "One Shot" are my favorites because each song speaks of overcoming fears and obstacles while taking the risk to live out your dreams and realize your full potential.

God led me to the song "Lord Knows" by Ace Hood during the darkest and most challenging financial experience my family has ever faced. My husband and I had both lost our jobs; we had exhausted our entire savings; we had a mountain of overdue bills; we were running out of food, and we didn't have the money to buy groceries. "Lord Knows" just appeared on the opening page of my favorite free music streaming website one day. I felt the Lord saying, "Listen to that song." I clicked on it, and the lyrics instantly spoke to me. They talk about how God does see and know our problems even through our darkest times.

This man had been through the very same struggles I was facing and had found his way out. It gave me a sense of hope that if he had gotten through his challenges, so could I. In his own way, this rapper reached out to the Lord and was brutally honest about his feelings. Even so, in the end, he was still talking to the Lord. God is big enough to handle our feelings. In the end, what He ultimately wants from us is a genuine, honest, and transparent relationship.

The more extreme or overt the manner in which the Lord reaches out to us signifies how important it is to Him that we recognize that He is speaking to us. The loudest I have heard the Lord communicate is when an agnostic spoke to my husband. My husband had a big dream in his heart, very personal and specific. I am the only person with whom he ever shared his dream. As the years passed, and the dream wasn't realized, the possibility of the dream's fulfillment appeared unrealistic. The dream was starting to fade from my husband's thoughts.

One day while we were having dinner with family, an agnostic family member excitedly pulled my husband aside to tell him about a dream he recently had. My husband was in his dream. With acute precision, he described every part of the dream the Lord had placed on my husband's heart down to the minutest detail. The Lord orchestrated things so that it was unmistakable that He was speaking. By speaking this way, God strongly captured my husband's attention and helped bring his dream back to life.

The Lord is constantly reaching out to us. The only real obstacle to unfettered communication with Him is attuning our hearts, minds, and senses to the myriad of ways that He is endlessly reaching out to us. Once you make that initial connection, it opens up an entire world of uninhibited and unstoppable communication. Look around and pay attention. How is the Lord trying to speak to you?

LESSON 5: WARRIOR

WHAT IMAGES DO THE WORD 'warrior' evoke in your mind? What actions, physical traits, or mindsets do you equate with someone who is a warrior? Do you consider a warrior to be a hero or someone almost super-human? What role, if any, do you believe being a warrior has to do with our spiritual life? And, if we believe we are warriors, what challenges would we face head on rather than trying to avoid?

A warrior is a person who fights in battles with courage and skill. For most people, I believe this conjures up images of fearlessness as well as traits and abilities that are beyond an average person's capabilities. I think this is due to courage as an attribute of a warrior. Many people believe that courage is the absence of fear. However, in reality, courage involves an element of fear.

The definition of courage says: "mental or moral strength to venture, persevere, and withstand danger, fear, or difficulty."[11] It is only through overcoming one's fears that we attain courage. By removing the notion that we cannot have courage without fear, the idea of becoming a warrior is now attainable. As Eleanor Roosevelt simply and clearly stated, "You gain strength, courage, and confidence by every experience in which

---

[11] *Merriam-Webster Dictionary*. 2017. "Courage." https://www.merriam-webster.com/dictionary/courage.

you really stop to look fear in the face. You must do the one thing which you think you cannot."[12]

The story of David and Goliath in 1 Samuel 17 exemplifies the courage it takes to face one's giants and adds an additional element, the belief that with God on your side, you cannot fail. Goliath was a man of giant proportions who fought for the Philistines. The Philistine army considered him their undefeatable weapon. Every day, Goliath taunted and terrorized the Israelite soldiers, tempting someone to have the courage to challenge him to one-on-one combat. The soldiers, looking through natural eyes, shrank back with fear.

David, a shepherd, was the youngest son in his family. He was looked down on and viewed as the least of his brothers. David's older brothers were fighting with the army. Between his duties of tending sheep, his father sent him to the front lines of the battle with provisions for his brothers. While delivering supplies, he witnessed Goliath belittle God and the army of Israel.

He was enraged that anyone dared to speak that way toward his God. So, he went to the tent of the king of Israel, Saul, and asked for permission to fight Goliath. Just like his family, King Saul looked at him and saw a seemingly feeble and inexperienced young man. He made several attempts to discourage David. But David knew from previous experience as a shepherd that God fought on his side. David said to Saul:

Your servant has been keeping his father's sheep. When a lion or a bear came and carried off a sheep from the flock, I went

---

[12] FDR Presidential Library & Museum. 2016. "Eleanor Roosevelt." https://fdrlibrary.org/eleanor-roosevelt.

after it, struck it and rescued the sheep from its mouth. When it turned on me, I seized it by its hair, struck it and killed it. Your servant has killed both the lion and the bear; this uncircumcised Philistine will be like one of them, because he has defied the armies of the living God. The LORD who rescued me from the paw of the lion and the paw of the bear will rescue me from the hand of this Philistine (1 Samuel 17:34-37, NIV).

When King Saul realized he could not persuade David to relent, he agreed to let him fight Goliath. He insisted that David use his armor and sword. However, David was not accustomed to protecting himself and his flock in this manner. To appease the king, he donned the armor, but it proved too heavy and ill-suited for him. David knew he had to face the giant with the tools of his trade—courage, belief in God, and his slingshot.

David's decision to fight Goliath his own way reveals another aspect of a seasoned warrior. A warrior knows they need to be true to themselves and use the arsenal of weapons they have mastered during their training with the Lord. To an outsider, these weapons or tools might appear worthless, lacking, or unsuitable. However, they don't realize that these tools have been personally customized and tailored for you by God. One of the biggest challenges a warrior for the Lord might face is advice from well-meaning individuals. A warrior knows that above all, they must do what they know to be right and fight every battle as the Lord leads them.

So, David faced Goliath the way he had faced every other challenge in his young life. With a mighty declaration of faith, he told the giant:

You come against me with sword and spear and javelin, but I come against you in the name of the LORD Almighty, the God of the armies of Israel, whom you have defied. This day the LORD will deliver you into my hands, and I'll strike you down and cut off your head. This very day I will give the carcasses of the Philistine army to the birds and the wild animals, and the whole world will know that there is a God in Israel. All those gathered here will know that it is not by sword or spear that the LORD saves; for the battle is the LORD's, and he will give all of you into our hands (1 Samuel 17:45-47, NIV).

And, just as he had spoken, David triumphed over the giant.

David was victorious over Goliath for a number of key reasons. The main reason he triumphed was because he trusted in the Lord and drew strength from Him. Second, David realized that with God fighting on his side, the only possible outcome was victory. Third, he reminded himself of all the times in his life that the Lord had proved Himself faithful. And last, he verbally declared that the victory was already his.

Whether he realized it or not, David was prophetically speaking a reality that was later revealed through Christ's resurrection. That reality is that Jesus has secured victory for everyone who trusts in Him.

What this means is that Jesus' work is finished. Christ secured victory and is now seated in a place of rest at the right hand of the Father. His work is done. He has already won every battle we will ever face in our lives. In the Garden of Gethsemane before He went to the cross, Jesus declared His finished work when He said to the disciples, "I have told you these things, so that in me you may have peace. In this world you will have trouble. But take heart! I have overcome the world" (John 16:33, NIV).

When the outcome is completely assured, that makes our work as warriors much easier. It means that all we need to do is follow the example set by David and stand firmly on the foundation of victory that has already been established for us. It is looking at the mountain in front of you and decreeing:

"God has already given this to me. I don't care how it looks. The victory is mine. I will stand on His promises and declare that victory until my circumstances match the truth of what God has promised me."

Standing in this posture is a declaration of faith, daring to see through spiritual eyes. It is the absolute belief that the Lord is for you and that the army He has fighting on your behalf is greater than anything coming against you.

This is illustrated in the story of Elisha and his servant. The King of Aram had sent an army to Dothan to capture Elisha. They surrounded the city during the night. Elisha's servant was afraid when he saw the army. But Elisha stood there unshakable and unmovable. Their interaction is described as follows:

When the servant of the man of God got up and went out early the next morning, an army with horses and chariots had surrounded the city. "Oh no, my lord! What shall we do?" the servant asked.

"Don't be afraid," the prophet answered. "Those who are with us are more than those who are with them."

And Elisha prayed, "Open his eyes, LORD, so that he may see." Then the LORD opened the servant's eyes, and he looked and saw the hills full of horses and chariots of fire all around Elisha (2 Kings 6:15-17, NIV).

Whether your spiritual eyes are open like Elisha or closed like his servant, you must face every challenge with faith. Our very thoughts and words instruct the unseen spiritual realm how to act on our behalf. The angels that the Lord provides to us during times of battle must follow our orders. We either enable them through our focus on faith and victory, or we disable them with our doubt and fear.

I recently watched a movie, *Tomorrowland,* with the central theme of the power of the thought and intention of a single person. The heroine, a teenage girl named Casey Newton, was able to save the world by believing things could be changed for the better. In the movie, the world is mere days away from complete destruction.

The source of the world's impending doom is the projection of the entire population's belief in the upcoming end of the world. The only person who is looking for solutions and believes that the world can be saved is Casey. The rest of the population is driven to wholeheartedly embrace their own destruction by a machine that is broadcasting their impending demise. The more the people embrace the message being broadcast to their subconscious, the more their thoughts and subsequent actions actually empower and create the doomsday message they have been fed.

Strangely enough, the people gravitate toward a message spreading doom. The viewer wonders why they wouldn't reject that message and choose hope instead. As the evil character, David Nix, who is broadcasting the negative message in hopes of destroying the earth, said, "In every moment there's the possibility of a better future, but you people won't believe it. And because you won't believe it you won't do what is necessary to make it a reality. So, you dwell on this terrible future. You resign yourselves to it for one reason, because that future does not ask anything of you today."[13]

The warrior must consciously choose hope over fear. Like Casey in the movie, they must look straight at their mountain of fear and lies and take actions today that will cost them something in return for a better future. The hardest challenge for any warrior is to stand and to continue standing in a posture of belief against all prevailing odds that they will be victorious. The warrior speaks the truth to their mountain and makes the mountain bend to their will.

So, how does all of this work in our everyday lives? I shared earlier that my husband and I had gone through a very harrowing financial downturn a few years ago. As a result of what we experienced, our credit was ruined. Just when we were getting back on our feet and thought that we were turning the corner, we were sued by one of our creditors.

I can't begin to describe the shock or the wave of abject fear that tried to overwhelm me when we were served with the lawsuit paperwork. The world started spinning, and it was all I could do to keep from losing it. The next morning, the Lord strongly impressed on me that He wanted me to get out of the house and go for a

---

[13] *The Internet Movie Database.* 2017. "Tomorrowland Quotes." http://m.imdb.com/title/tt1964418/quotes?item=qt2498059.

long walk. I was pouring my heart out to God when something on the sidewalk in front of me caught my eye—graffiti.

However, this wasn't your typical graffiti. When I stopped in front of it, I saw the words, "**Be Won**." An angel's halo was drawn around the top of the "w" in the word "won." I started to calm down. I kept walking and turned left at the next corner. There, in front of me again, was the "**Be Won**" graffiti. At this point, I had to laugh out loud. I knew the battle I was facing had just begun, but God was making it extremely clear that He had already won the battle on my behalf. From that moment on, the instant that fear or anxiety tried to creep up on me, I announced in my head, "Be won. This battle has already been won!"

My husband and I had a very steep and short learning curve. We had to learn legal terms, research the documents we needed to file, and find a lawyer. Early on, our only option was clearly to file bankruptcy.

Since my husband was working full-time, I had to handle most of the trips to the courthouse and the appointments with our lawyer. Paperwork had to be filed with the court a week before Christmas. During an already hectic and stressful time of year, I made three trips to the courthouse. I will admit, I was terrified each time I had to go downtown.

I had never been to the main courthouse before, which was huge, intimidating, and impersonal. Homeless and mentally unstable people camped out in the alleys and side-streets around the courthouse. Walking past them to take care of my paperwork filled me with fear and dread as I thought that my family could end up in the same situation as these poor people. I felt like a loser and a complete failure.

The culmination of our filing was a meeting between us, our lawyer, and a court-appointed trustee. We had to provide all the documentation pertaining to our bankruptcy filing and answer any questions the trustee had. This court-appointed officer had the final say on whether or not our bankruptcy filing was valid. One document was missing from our file, and the trustee asked for clarification on another document.

A second meeting was scheduled. My husband was unable to take another day off work, so this time I had to face the trustee alone. Completely terrified and feeling like a tiny coward, I met our lawyer at the court building and provided the requested information. We were victorious, and our bankruptcy was approved.

As we were preparing to leave the building, our lawyer thanked me for being part of the process, having a positive attitude, providing everything needed, and actually attending the meetings. He then looked at me and stated, "You're a warrior." Up until this point, I had felt like anything but a warrior. I felt like a fearful coward. His statement helped me realize the true meaning of a warrior. I had faced one of the scariest experiences of my life, but I kept going, and I had come through the other side victorious because I did not quit.

Often, when the Lord is ready to promote us, He asks us to face challenges that we need to overcome in our lives in order to handle the next level successfully. In the struggling and grappling, the Lord draws hidden abilities that have been lying dormant deep within us to the surface. As written for the film, *Voyage of the Dawn*

Treader, "Hardships often prepare ordinary people for an extraordinary destiny."[14]

A few years ago, I had an interesting dialog with the Lord one morning. I had recently come out of a series of challenging seasons and found myself avoiding anything that appeared difficult or painful. The Lord strongly impressed upon me that He didn't view circumstances in the same way that people did. He doesn't consider the same things painful that we do. We had an inaccurate perception of what was painful or bad.

The very things that people desperately avoid were actually opportunities for Him to heal us, set us free, and accomplish incredible things in our lives. Suddenly, I was no longer afraid of the future. I felt a peace beyond anything I could express. I became excited that the Lord could use anything for my good because my perspective had changed. I had deemed situations as negative because they made me uncomfortable, when in reality the Lord was using them for my own benefit.

What if we had an accurate perspective of what it means to be a warrior? What would we not be afraid to face? When God called us to new heights, how would we respond differently? God always speaks to our potential and to our hidden strengths. He calls us out into the deep with Him because He knows how it ends. He doesn't call us until He knows we're ready. He prepares us with each battle for the next stage of our journey. Each

---

[14] *The C.S. Lewis Foundation.* 2017. "Quotes Often Misattributed to C.S. Lewis." http://www.cslewis.org/aboutus/faq/quotes-misattributed/.

exercise strengthens us and hones the skills we'll need at the next level.

When God looks at you, He sees a warrior. He sees you more accurately than you see yourself. He knows that you are braver than you think. And He knows the army He sends to fight on your behalf will be victorious. Now, go and conquer that mountain God has given you!

LESSON 6: OVERCOME

WHAT DOES IT MEAN TO be an overcomer? What are the characteristics of an overcomer? What differentiates an overcomer from a survivor? How would we live our lives differently with an overcomer mindset?

An overcomer is someone who comes out of a challenging situation stronger, better, and without scars. The definition of the root word "overcome" includes elements of surmounting, overwhelming, defeating, and winning. The overcomer prevails against any and every circumstance, difficulty, or weakness with their faith intact and without detrimental changes to them as a result of what they have endured.

In contrast, a survivor is someone who comes out of a situation with a scar, a scar that stays with them. That scar alters their behavior and who they are for the rest of their lives. They come out of the situation without letting it completely destroy them, but they are intrinsically changed, and they carry around a daily reminder of their pain. In essence, they carry a wound, their hurt, and that situation forever.

At any time, a survivor can become an overcomer by allowing the Lord to come in and reveal the truth of the situation they have misinterpreted as a result of the pain of their experience. In order to gain freedom from their past, they have to come to a place where they no longer want to stay in their current condition. Simply put, the pain of where they are has to become greater than the pain of change. As soon as they are willing to go through the healing process with the Lord, He can remove their scar and transform them into an overcomer.

The Bible relates numerous examples of overcomers: Abraham, Joseph, Esther, David, Peter, and the Apostle Paul, to name just a few. Anyone the Lord has used for great things allowed Him to use the circumstances in their lives to shape them for their God-given destiny. The story of Ruth and Naomi takes a unique look at an overcomer and a survivor who is transformed into an overcomer.

Naomi, her husband, and two sons left Jerusalem during a famine and went to Moab. The people of Moab worshiped other Gods. Shortly after arriving, Naomi's husband died. Her two sons married Moabite women. Ten years later, both of Naomi's sons died, leaving her alone. The famine in Israel had ended, and Naomi prepared to return home.

Naomi urged her daughter-in-laws to stay in Moab and return to their families and traditions. She told them, "No, my daughters. It is more bitter for me than for you, because the LORD's hand has turned against me" (Ruth 1: 13b, NIV)! Naomi felt they had a greater chance of remarrying and having a better life without her in their native country. However, her daughter-in-law, Ruth, refused to leave her side. So the two women journeyed back to Bethlehem, arriving at the beginning of the barley harvest.

Naomi and Ruth's arrival in Bethlehem caused quite a stir.

So the two women went on until they came to Bethlehem. When they arrived in Bethlehem, the whole town was stirred because of them, and the women exclaimed, "Can this be Naomi?"

"Don't call me Naomi," she told them. "Call me Mara, because the Almighty has made my life very bitter. I went away full, but the LORD has brought me back empty. Why call me Naomi? The LORD has afflicted me; the Almighty has brought misfortune upon me" (Ruth 1:19b-20a, NIV).

This is the second time that Naomi has stated that her life is bitter. She again accuses God of being against her. She was so distraught that she asked to be called "Mara," which means "bitter." She changed her name to something tragic to constantly remind herself of her pain. Also of note is the fact that the women of the town no longer even recognized the woman who returned.

Naomi had a relative from her husband's family named Boaz, an important man in Bethlehem. Ruth went out into a field behind the harvesters with the hope to "pick up the leftover grain behind anyone in whose eyes I find favor" (Ruth 2:2, NIV). However, unlike Naomi, Ruth believed that she would find favor. Just like Naomi, she had also lost everything, but Ruth chose to cling to hope and faith.

Ruth was gleaning from a field belonging to Boaz. When Boaz learned who she was, he had the following interaction with Ruth:

So Boaz said to Ruth, "My daughter, listen to me. Don't go and glean in another field and don't go away from here. Stay here with the women who work for me. Watch the field where the men are harvesting, and follow along after the women. I have told the men not to lay a hand on you. And whenever you are thirsty, go and get a drink from the water jars the men have filled."

At this, she bowed down with her face to the ground. She asked him, "Why have I found such favor in your eyes that you notice me — a foreigner?"

Boaz replied, "I've been told all about what you have done for your mother-in-law since the death of your husband — how you left your father and mother and your homeland and came to live with a people you did not know before. May the LORD repay you for what you have done. May you be richly rewarded by the LORD, the God of Israel, under whose wings you have come to take refuge."

"May I continue to find favor in your eyes, my lord," she said. "You have put me at ease by speaking kindly to your servant — though I do not have the standing of one of your servants" (Ruth 2:8-13, NIV).

Boaz chose to show great favor and bestow blessings upon Ruth because of her faithfulness to Naomi. He allowed her to glean in his fields and instructed his men to leave her alone; this was an act of kindness on his part to help keep her safe. Boaz also instructed his harvesters to intentionally leave extra grain and stalks behind for her to gather.

Boaz was not only a close relative of Naomi's family, he was also a guardian-redeemer. This meant that he had a familial right to redeem a relative who was in serious difficulty, according to Levitical law. Naomi could not take care of Ruth long-term and realized that she needed to find a home for her. She knew that, according to their tradition, Boaz could be prevailed upon to redeem them by purchasing the land that belonged to her husband. In addition, he would also have the right to take Ruth as his wife.

Naomi understood how Ruth could communicate her intentions to Boaz so that he would act as their guardian-redeemer and marry Ruth. She gave Ruth instructions to dress in her finest clothes and find Boaz at the threshing floor in the evening after he was merry from eating and drinking. She also told Ruth to uncover his feet and lay down next to him.

Without complete understanding, Ruth trusted her mother-in-law and did as she said. All overcomers have to take leaps of faith and trust that, whether or not their actions make sense, the situation will work out.

Boaz woke in the middle of the night to find Ruth at his feet. As instructed by Naomi, Ruth spoke. "'I am your servant, Ruth,'" she said. 'Spread the corner of your garment over me since you are a guardian-redeemer of our family.'" Boaz understood the meaning of this gesture.

He was moved by her actions and resolved to do his duty. However, a closer relative than him was due first chance to act as the guardian-redeemer. He took the proposal to this man, who was unable to redeem the land. Ruth then became his wife and bore him a son.

Ruth's marriage to Boaz and the birth of her son was a turning point for Naomi. The Lord redeemed her and everything she had lost. In the process, He transformed Naomi into an overcomer. No longer did she cling to the pain of her past. Instead, filled with hope, she cared for Ruth's baby as if he were her own son.

Ruth's child was Obed, the grandfather of David. Later in history, Jesus was born from the line of David. As a result of her faithfulness, God saw in Ruth the qualities He wanted in His own lineage. God used her as part of the family line of the greatest king in the history of Israel and the Savior of mankind.

There have been countless numbers of overcomers throughout history. Corrie ten Boom was imprisoned in a Nazi camp for hiding Jews during World War II.

Despite the atrocities she endured and the horror she witnessed, she made it out alive with her hope and faith in God still intact. She spent the remainder of her life traveling the world to spread the message that "there is no pit so deep, that God's love is not still deeper."[15]

Desmond Doss is another example of an overcomer from World War II. He went to war, refusing to carry a weapon, choosing instead to be a medic in hopes of saving lives instead of taking them. For years, he was ridiculed by the other soldiers and his superiors. One commander went so far as to even try to have him kicked out of the military.

However, with God's help, he prevailed in that battle as well as in the battle of Hacksaw Ridge in the Pacific. Single-handedly over the course of one night, Desmond Doss saved seventy-five soldiers during one of the most brutal campaigns of the war. Some of the men he saved were the very soldiers who had treated him so cruelly.

He is the only conscientious objector to receive the Congressional Medal of Honor. Ironically, the very

---

[15] ten Boon, Corrie. 1971 and 1984. *The Hiding Place*. Grand Rapids, MI. Chosen Books.

soldiers that tried to have him kicked out of the army recommended him for the Medal of Honor.[16]

Joyce Meyer is a modern-day example. She experienced a horrific childhood filled with abuse. She started out as a survivor struggling for years as a result of the pain she experienced growing up and into her early adult years. However, she persevered and spent years diligently working with the Lord to overcome her past and live in freedom. Then, the Lord called her into ministry at a time when very few women ministers were preaching the Gospel. More than thirty years later, Joyce Meyer runs a ministry with worldwide outreach, has a daily program on mainstream television, and has written numerous books.

A single thread weaves a common theme throughout each narrative of every overcomer throughout history— holding on to faith in the midst of adversity and the unknown and continuing to trust the Lord when He asks us to do things that don't make sense. As Martin Luther King, Jr said, "Faith is taking the first step, even when you don't see the whole staircase."[17]

This reminds me of a scene from the movie, *Indiana Jones and the Last Crusade*. Indiana Jones and his father are

---

[16] *People*. Miller, Mike. Feb. 24, 2017. "The True Story of Hacksaw Ridge and Desmond Doss: the Medal of Honor Winner Who Never Fired a Shot." http://people.com/movies/the-true-story-of-hacksaw-ridge-and-desmond-doss-the-medal-of-honor-winner-who-never-fired-a-shot/.

[17] *Martin Luther King, Jr.'s Civil Rights Dream*. King, Martin Luther, Jr. Accessed July 17, 2017. "I Have a Dream." https://sites.google.com/a/bnths.nthls.com/spartans2014civilrights/home/ihaveadreamspeech.

searching for the Holy Grail, which is the cup that Jesus drank from at the Last Supper as well as the cup used by Joseph of Arimathea to collect Jesus' blood when He was crucified. They are mere steps away from the room that holds the grail. However, an immense chasm separates them from that room with no bridge in sight.

At this point, the villain shoots the father to force Indiana Jones into retrieving the grail to save his father's life. Indiana steps to the edge of the precipice and looks at the entrance to the room that contains the grail he so desperately needs. Suddenly, he remembers a painting he had seen in his father's house. The painting depicted a knight reaching his hands toward a chalice while walking suspended in mid-air over a chasm.

Indiana gulped, summoned the courage to believe, and took that precarious first step. Rather than plummeting to his death, he was surprised to find his foot land firmly on something solid. As he took another step, a bridge appeared. He was able to cross over, retrieve the grail, and save his father because of that first step of faith.

Just like in the movie, the Lord has already gone before us and made a way. However, that path is often hidden from our natural eyes until we take that first step, and our act of faith begins to illuminate the next step of our journey. The overcomer has the faith to step out into the unknown because they know the one who holds their future is faithful.

Every overcomer has gone through harrowing and difficult circumstances. As it says in James 1:2-4, "Consider it pure joy, my brothers and sisters, whenever you face trials of many kinds, because you know that the testing of your faith produces perseverance. Let perseverance finish its work so that you may be mature and complete, not lacking anything" (NIV). Through the very act of overcoming and the testimony they have to share, these people can encourage others.

The qualities that an overcomer possesses that enable them to persevere include:

- Trusting the Lord enough to go through the trial
- Holding on to faith in the midst of the trial
- Believing that they have the Lord's favor
- Knowing that the Lord has made a way through for them
- Staying positive
- Declaring victory and
- Never giving up.

Although the examples I've shared are of great people throughout history, the Lord leads everyone this way. In our everyday ordinary lives, the Lord presents opportunities for us to overcome with His help. In this way, the Lord has helped me overcome many things in my life.

For the first eleven years of our married life, the enemy did everything possible to destroy our marriage. Two breaking points came for me when I thought I couldn't go on anymore, and I wanted to leave my husband. The first time, the Lord spoke to me through a counselor and asked me to stay. The second time, the Lord spoke to me directly.

The second breaking point happened in the midst of a heated argument, and I threatened to leave my husband. The Lord very clearly and sternly warned me, "You don't want to do this!" This was not what I wanted to hear from Him, and I was angry. I have always been obedient to the Lord no matter what is has cost me, and I knew I would obey this request. But in this instance, I decided I was going to obey on my terms, not the Lord's. I told the Lord that I would stay but that He couldn't make me love my husband or be kind to him. I also told the Lord that I no longer trusted Him and that I was going to protect myself.

The instant that I decided to protect myself, a wall began building around my heart. At first, I felt safe behind my self-made barrier. I was under the delusion that I was merely protecting myself from continuing to be hurt in my marriage. What I didn't realize at the time was that I had inadvertently also blocked the Lord from complete access to my heart. Over time, I felt less and less, less love and less life, yet, somehow, the pain not only continued, it intensified.

When I threatened to leave my husband, I didn't realize that the Lord used that to start the healing process. My husband realized a serious issue in our marriage was hurting me. He also began to understand that his choices and actions not only affected his life but also my life and the lives of our children. These two realizations began a healing process for him with the Lord. For years, the Lord secretly worked on my husband's heart, and things began to change. I also did not know that at the same time the Lord asked me to stay, He asked my husband to love me no matter what I did or how I treated him.

I thought the cross I had to bear for the rest of my life was the pain in our marriage. For years, the pain and suffering of our marriage was an open and festering wound in my heart. Every day, it felt as if the scab to my wound was being torn off and as if salt was poured in it. I became a bitter, ugly, and resentful person with the sole object of going after my husband. I wanted him to be as bitter and resentful as I was. Yet, no matter how ugly I was to my husband, he was loving and kind to me.

Unexpectedly, three years after I threatened to leave, the Lord completely removed the issue in our marriage that made me want to leave. For nearly two years following that, my husband worked very diligently with the Lord to fix the areas in his heart and life that needed healing. Whenever the Lord shows my husband an area in his life that needs correction, he instantly and wholeheartedly works with the Lord. It doesn't matter what the cost might be or the temporary pain and discomfort during the healing process, my husband commits to change and does whatever is necessary. He would rather know the truth and be set free than continue in a dysfunctional but comfortable lie. It is one of the qualities that I admire most about my husband.

My husband was healed, but I still had a massive and infected scar. Over the years, I had come to believe that I was justified in holding on to my anger because of the pain I had gone through. It was my friend and my companion. I felt that if I let it go, it would mean that what I had gone through was meaningless and had been for nothing.

I didn't realize that my pain was a cancer that was hurting me. As a result of holding on to my pain, I was inflicting damage to my marriage. I was so focused on the perceived wrongs of my husband that I was blind to my own bad behavior toward him.

Then, the Lord started broaching the subject of forgiveness. I hate to admit that it took me a long time to come to the place where I could sincerely forgive, let go, and move on. When I was truly able to forgive my husband, I was transformed from a survivor to an overcomer.

I expected things in our marriage to instantly improve. However, as soon as I forgave my husband, I truly saw for the first time how ugly and wrong I had been. I was terrified to see the damage I had caused to our marriage. I had to humbly work to reconcile with my husband and to regain his trust. It took a long time to mend the damage I had caused. After that, our marriage was truly healthy and better than it had ever been.

Now, many years later, we are still happy. They have been the best and most joyful years we have ever shared together, even during challenging circumstances in life. With each passing year, our marriage grows stronger.

The overcomer lives in the knowledge that, "I can do all things through Christ who strengthens me" (Philippians 4:13, NKJV). They are keenly aware that, because of the indwelling of Christ within them, they also have the power and authority to overcome this world, and we gain victory in this world through faith.

It doesn't matter if you're a survivor and the embers of hope that fuel the fire of your dream are on the verge of going out. You were born an overcomer. At any moment, you can be transformed into an overcomer, and your embers can be fanned back into a burning flame. If you're an overcomer, continue standing in faith. Continue in the strength of the Lord, knowing that you are a light to those who are merely surviving.

Whatever dreams you have ever had for your life originated from the Lord. The challenges you have faced in the pursuit of achieving your dreams have really been opportunities in disguise for the Lord to help you realize what you are truly capable of achieving. You have the power within you to overcome and transform this world for the better.

LESSON 7: GRACE

THE WORD "GRACE" OFTEN ELICITS a varied range of emotions. Our interpretation depends on our experience with grace received in our life. By its very nature and definition, grace is not something we can create for ourselves. The definition of the word includes elements such as: favor, goodwill, and mercy. And, in terms of theology, grace is God's freely given, unmerited favor and love.

Grace can often seem elusive because it cannot be achieved through human efforts. The fact that it can't be bought or earned is what makes it so priceless and enduring. In the end, this ultimately makes it easy to attain once we are willing to let go and stop our striving. Scottish preacher Alexander Whyte captured the simplicity and power of the concept of grace when he said, "And as grace is free, so is it sure. Nothing can change, or alter, or turn away sovereign grace."[18]

What exactly is grace? What does it look like? How do we recognize it in our own lives? Recognizing grace operating in our daily lives comes down to understanding the true nature of God. At His very core, God is love; every action He takes is out of love for His children. Closely tied to love is God's desire for relationship. Every parent desires to have a loving, meaningful, rich, and intimate relationship with their children. God is no different.

---

[18] Whyte, Alexander. 1903. *The Apostle Paul*. Edinburgh, Scotland.

To recognize grace, we must first recognize how the Lord interacts with us. He cannot and will not violate our free will. Every action He takes will be guided by love and with our best interest at the core. God will reach out to us in limitless ways, yet His manner will include the following core elements:

- God operates differently than the world
- God speaks about potential rather than sin
- God creates an environment where being with Him is the safest place and
- God focuses on forgiveness.

God Operates Differently than the World

God doesn't do things the way the world does. He doesn't keep count of the things you do wrong and bring them up every time you mess up. God also does not disqualify you when you do something wrong. As a friend once shared with my husband, "You do not lose your place in line. You start from the exact same spot." Basically, when you miss the mark and go off on your own, God patiently waits for you to realize that you can't do it on your own and come back to Him for help. He doesn't chastise you and make you start all over; no, He starts moving you forward from your last position with Him.

In that case, if God doesn't punish us, how does He handle sin? With grace, He loves you and redeems you from your mistakes. Whenever I have messed up, the Lord goes out of His way to bless me in some unexpected way. I know when I've missed the mark, and I am hard on myself when I know I haven't behaved as I should. Within hours, the Lord usually shows me His favor through one or more of the following: random acts of kindness, others who go out of their way to be gracious and generous, encouraging words or pictures, or significant images, such as rainbows and hawks. This is God's way of reminding me that He knows who I am and that I will always have His blessing and favor in my life. His gentle overtures toward me quickly help me to let go of self-accusation and guilt and return to acting like myself.

A more poignant example happened to my husband when he was a young adult. He was new in his relationship with the Lord. He was doing things that weren't pleasing to the Lord and living a lifestyle he knew he shouldn't. Every day, he thought, "I wonder if this is going to be the day the Lord is going to call me out on my behavior." He thought the Lord would bring up his actions and deal with him about his life. But the Lord never did.

Instead, every day, the Lord reached out to him with love and grace. Six months later, my husband decided on his own that he didn't want to keep living his life that way. That lifestyle no longer demonstrated who he was. The desire for that lifestyle completely left him, and he changed his life. Guilt and shame would have kept him trapped in unhealthy patterns. The Lord showed him love and mercy. He was transformed by the Lord's grace.

God Speaks about Potential rather than Sin

Sin has its own consequences, and God allows us to experience those consequences. He does not heap any blame, shame, guilt, or condemnation on top of our bad choices. The Lord seeks to redeem us out of our mistakes and help us to rebuild. In addition, He once spoke to me through my daughter and said, "I will even use some of your mistakes to help bless you."

Another time, after my husband did something that he considered to be his biggest failure, the Lord told him that what he did was a tiny anthill in His eyes. The Lord also told my husband that he was taking something that He considered to be minor and blowing it out of proportion and turning it into a mountain. Since He could see my husband's life from start to finish, the Lord knew that this incident was insignificant in the scheme of the things he would accomplish over his life as well as in the face of the Lord's grace.

God is perfectly able to take the very things that you have consciously or inadvertently done wrong and use them to bless you. Two examples from the Bible perfectly illustrate the Lord's grace: the stories of the woman caught in adultery and when Peter denied Christ.

Jesus was teaching in the Temple. While he was teaching, the Pharisees and teachers of the religious law brought in a woman who was caught in the act of adultery. They told Jesus that the law called for her to be stoned. Trying to trick him into saying something that they could use against him, they asked him, "What do you say?" (John 8:5, NLT)

Jesus had stooped down to write in the sand and was ignoring the religious leaders. They kept demanding that he answer. Finally, he stood up and said, "'All right, but let the one who has never sinned throw the first stone'" (John 8:7, NLT). He then stooped down again to write in the sand.

Hearing Jesus' words, the accusers quietly slipped away one at a time, starting with the oldest. Jesus was left alone with the woman. He stood up again and said to her:

"'Where are your accusers? Didn't even one of them condemn you?'"

"'No, Lord,' she said."

"And Jesus said, 'Neither do I. Go and sin no more'" (John 8:10b-11, NLT).

Notice the very different responses. Those who lived by and upheld the law wanted the harshest punishment allowable by law to be carried out. They felt justified in their response because by all outward appearances, they were blameless and sinless pillars of the community. However, it was very telling that the oldest, those with the most sin in their lives, were the first to slink away.

In contrast, Jesus, the only sinless and blameless person there, showed the woman mercy, grace, and compassion. By all accounts, her sin was publicly known, yet Jesus refused to heap further condemnation upon her. He knew that the only way to redeem her and offer her a fresh start in life was to offer her forgiveness.

As alluded to earlier by the response of the Pharisees, religion focuses on sin. So does the enemy. Martin Luther, who was one of the first to publicly speak out and advocate for change in the church, witnessed and experienced firsthand the crippling effects of a system focused on sin and the law. As he noted, "The law works fear and wrath; grace works hope and mercy."[19]

Luther was a monk, scholar, and theologian. Even so, as time passed, he felt his relationship with the Lord change and diminish as if God was farther and more removed from his life. According to religious tradition, sin was the issue and could be rooted out by certain works in order to earn one's salvation. Early on as a monk, Martin Luther spent many long hours in prayer, confession, and self-scourging.

He did all this in attempts to draw closer to the Lord. It didn't help, so he increased the intensity, frequency, and length of his self-purification. But this activity had the opposite result. The more he focused on sin, the more distant God seemed from his life. Luther described this period of his life, saying, "I lost touch with Christ the Savior and Comforter, and made of him the jailer and hangman of my poor soul."[20]

Over time, Luther turned his focus from his sins back to Christ. He came to realize that true repentance did not involve penance and self-inflicted punishments but rather a change of heart. Through careful study and meditation on Scripture, Luther was pointed toward the Lord's grace and mercy.

This shift in emphasis from sin to God's grace and mercy was a pivotal moment in Luther's life and the impetus that started him to question certain religious practices,

---

[19] Luther, Martin, edited by Atkinson, James. 1962. *Early theological works: Volume 16 of Library of Christian classics*. The University of Michigan, Ann Arbor, Michigan. Westminister Press.
[20] Luther, Martin. 1580. *Book of Concord*. Dresden, Germany.

traditions, and beliefs, in particular, the church's corrupt practice of selling indulgences, a means by which one could purchase salvation. This questioning ultimately led Luther to the understanding that we only receive salvation through the Lord's divine grace by our faith in Him and not through works or deeds.

Martin Luther published his new-found beliefs in a document called the *Ninety-five Theses*, in which he questioned the church's practice of selling indulgences. This manuscript and the related beliefs threatened the church, their power, their ability to control people, and their finances. The church tried to persecute Luther and eventually resorted to trying to have him killed.

The church's efforts to eradicate Luther's growing influence over popular culture failed. His ideas grew and spread, ultimately becoming the catalyst for the Protestant Reformation. Luther's beliefs forever changed not only Christianity but also the course of Western history.

Religion seeks to keep people focused on sin to exert control over them. The enemy uses sin to disable people and keep them trapped in seemingly hopeless situations, ensuring that they will not be a threat to him. The biggest threat to the enemy is people who recognize their position with God as well as the power and freedom available to them through the Lord's grace.

How would you live differently if you were grace-conscious? If you live in the power of grace, you cannot help but transform those around you. You will seek to uplift and see the best in others. And, like Christ, you will be able to speak into people's lives to help pull them up out of the muck and mire.

The Lord's redemption of Peter is a strong example of the use of grace to set someone free from the bondage of guilt in order to enable them to fulfill their God-given destiny. Jesus and the disciples had just shared their last supper together. After dinner they went to the Mount of Olives. On the way there, Jesus told the disciples:

"All of you will desert me. For the Scriptures say,

*'God will strike the Shepherd,
and the sheep will be scattered.'*

But after I am raised from the dead, I will go ahead of you to Galilee and meet you there."

Peter said to him, "Even if everyone else deserts you, I never will."

Jesus replied, "I tell you the truth, Peter — this very night, before the rooster crows twice, you will deny three times that you even know me."

"No!" Peter declared emphatically. "Even if I have to die with you, I will never deny you!" And all the others vowed the same (Mark 14:27-31, NLT).

Jesus was speaking about future events. He was prophetically foretelling his death, resurrection, and the temporary scattering of his disciples in fear. When Peter could not believe that he was capable of deserting his Lord, Jesus had to tell him the hard truth that Peter would deny Him multiple times.

That very night, Jesus was arrested and taken to the home of the high priest. Peter followed them at a distance. The guards lit a fire in the courtyard, and Peter joined those who were sitting around the fire. In the light of the fire, a servant girl recognized him as a follower of

Jesus and confronted him. Peter's response was his first denial. A while later, someone else noticed him and accused him of being a disciple. Peter responded with his second denial.

Not long after this, someone else recognized that Peter was a Galilean. And for the third time, someone insisted that Peter was a follower of Jesus. Peter responded:

"Man, I don't know what you are talking about." And immediately, while he was still speaking, the rooster crowed.

At that moment the Lord turned and looked at Peter. Suddenly, the Lord's words flashed through Peter's mind: "Before the rooster crows tomorrow morning, you will deny three times that you even knew me." And Peter left the courtyard, weeping bitterly (Luke 22:60-62, NLT).

As Jesus had prophesied, Peter denied him three times. The Peter who fled the courtyard was not the confident man who had declared his undying devotion mere hours before. The man who left was broken and devastated by the realization that he had denied the person who meant everything to him. He was a shell of his former self.

After His resurrection, Jesus appeared to the disciples a handful of times before ascending to heaven. He appeared to a group of seven disciples, including Peter, next to the Sea of Galilee.

The disciples were out in a boat fishing when a man they did not recognize appeared along the shore. The man asked if they had caught any fish, and they replied that they hadn't. He told them to cast their net to the right of the boat. When they did as he said, the net became so full of fish that they had trouble hauling it in the boat.

At this point, John recognized that it was the Lord and told Peter. As soon as he heard the news, Peter jumped into the water and swam to shore while the rest of the disciples brought in the haul of fish. On shore, the disciples found breakfast waiting for them.

After breakfast, Jesus spoke to Peter saying:

"Simon son of John, do you love me more than these?"

"Yes, Lord," Peter replied, "you know I love you."

"Then feed my lambs," Jesus told him.

Jesus repeated the question: "Simon son of John, do you love me?"

"Yes, Lord," Peter said, "you know I love you."

"Then take care of my sheep," Jesus said.

A third time he asked him, "Simon son of John, do you love me?"

Peter was hurt that Jesus asked the question a third time. He said, "Lord, you know everything. You know that I love you."

Jesus said, "Then feed my sheep" (John 21:15-17, NLT).

With every iteration of the same question, the Lord was covering each of Peter's denials with grace. He was also reminding Peter of the call upon his life. Peter was the first person, through divine revelation, to recognize Jesus as the Messiah and Son of God. "Upon this rock" of Peter's divine revelation and profession of faith in Him as Christ that Jesus said, "I will build my church, and all the powers of hell will not conquer it" (Matthew 16:18, NLT).

The call of Peter's life was to care for and spiritually feed the flock of Christ's people who are His church. Jesus knew when He spoke this over Peter that he would betray him in the near future. But Peter's denials did not diminish or alter the call on his life. Jesus knew that Peter's faith was a firm foundation to build upon and that He would be able to restore him through grace. Peter never lost his place or position with Jesus. And because of that, he was able to carry out the immense calling on his life.

God Creates an Environment where the Safest Place is with Him

The safest place to be is in the Father's arms. Understanding grace is knowing the depth of the Father's love and that He desires relationship with us above all else. We have the courage to go to Him after any failure and be truly honest with Him.

At times, both my husband and I have gone to the Lord in anger and frustration over difficult circumstances and have been brutally honest with Him about how we were feeling. When I say, "brutal," I mean to the point of screaming, yelling, and swearing at God. He is big enough that He can handle my feelings.

One such occasion occurred during the difficult period in my marriage that I shared about earlier. I was very pregnant, and my baby was due any day. Things were reaching a boiling point in our lives.

My husband and I had a horrible fight. I was so upset and distraught that I decided to go for a walk in the heat of the day during the middle of summer. Our housing development was still being built up, so I went to a house that had just been framed and sat on the front steps in the shade of the structure. I picked this location because I knew that it would be quiet and deserted in the late afternoon.

As I sat there, I started crying. My sorrow quickly turned to anger, in particular, anger toward God. I had been crying out to Him for help for years, but nothing was changing. I couldn't understand why He continued to ask me to stay in my marriage without any help. And, then, I started audibly yelling and swearing at God.

I cried and screamed myself out until I was utterly exhausted. I finally calmed down and made one final plea to God. I was barely holding on to hope, and I desperately needed certain words of comfort and encouragement to keep going. I asked God for what I needed. When I heard silence, I got up and started walking back to my house, expecting to come home to a frustrated husband.

When I got home, my husband was waiting for me. As soon as I walked through the door, he apologized and took me in his arms. My husband said that while I was gone, the Lord started speaking to him about me and told him that he needed to tell me certain things. He then spoke the very words I had told God I needed to hear.

Just minutes earlier, I had been bitterly angry and cursing at God. However, He surprised me by His reaction. In the most beautiful and significant way, God used my husband to show me His grace. The Lord's response showed the depth of His love and care for both of us.

After all, He already knows what I'm feeling. If I try to hide my true feelings, the only person I am fooling is myself. Every time I have acted out this way toward the

Lord, He always surprised me by responding with grace, patience, and understanding.

Several years ago, the Lord gave me and my husband an object lesson on grace. When our dog was three years old, she completely tore away the ligaments around one of her knees, requiring knee-replacement surgery and a four-month recovery period where she could only get up to eat or to go to the bathroom. For such a young dog, being immobile for nearly twenty-four hours a day for months was torture.

During her recovery, though, the Lord individually taught both of us a unique lesson on grace. I witnessed the aspect of trust. She was in a lot of pain following her surgery, which later lessened to discomfort. When her pain subsided, she was left annoyed and frustrated at being forced to be immobile.

She looked up at me from her resting place on the floor one day, clearly hurt and sad. She unmistakably wanted me to know how she felt. She seemed to be saying through her eyes, "I don't know why you did this to me!" However, I also saw her saying in her eyes, "But I am choosing to still trust you."

I was honestly moved to tears. At the time, our family was going through a difficult and challenging season, so I understood how our dog felt. What moved me, though, was her stance of faith in us. She continued to trust us and look to us for help.

What she didn't understand was that we had acted out of love for her. As I realized this, I gained a greater understanding of God's grace toward us. Understanding how our dog felt helped me to have grace toward her. This perspective also further cemented in my mind how important it is to continue trusting God and going to Him, especially when we don't understand what He is currently doing in our life.

My husband had a separate lesson on how the Lord is always acting on our behalf. Once her intense pain subsided, our dog did everything she could to show her displeasure and anger toward us. With a cone around her head and limited mobility options, she had to find creative ways to misbehave. Somehow, she managed! She purposely hit things with her cone, often multiple times, sniffed for an eternity before going potty, resisted going inside, and on special occasions, resorted to peeing on the floor where she was lying.

When our dog misbehaved, my husband and I had grace for her because she had no idea that what we had done was to help her and vastly improve her quality of life. What resonated most with my husband was that our dog's behavior stemmed out of a misperception and lack of understanding. Witnessing this, my husband had a greater appreciation for the fact that, often, we don't see things happening in our lives because the Lord is doing things behind the scenes.

In return, he had a glimpse into how God sees things for His children and relates to them. In this instance, my husband was able to see from the start to the finish for our dog as God does. He could also empathize with her lack of understanding. Knowing the purpose for her temporary discomfort, my husband extended grace to our dog. Many times, he reached down, lovingly petted her, and said, "I know you don't understand. We did this because we love you, and your life will be better."

Isn't this exactly how the Lord responds to us when we're in the midst of confusion, doubt, or tantrums because we don't understand what He is doing? The Lord knows what He is doing, how it will end in our favor, and that our current behavior stems from a lack of understanding. In response, He wraps us up in the arms of His grace, soothes our fears, and encourages us to continue trusting Him.

Unbelievably, a little over a year later, our dog blew out her other knee, requiring a second surgery. But this time, she behaved quite differently. While she did not enjoy the surgery, she understood that, on the other side of her recovery she would be healed and have her life back better than it was before. There were no protests or bad behavior. She quietly and peacefully went through the process of recovery. This time around, the process didn't seem so difficult and also seemed to go by much more quickly.

The difference between our dog's first and second surgery recoveries were vastly different. Her first recovery was more stressful because she did not understand our intentions and acted out in hurt and frustration. The second time around, she knew we were helping her and worked with us to make her recovery as smooth and as easy as possible.

This was yet another lesson from the Lord. We have the choice to fight the Lord when He brings necessary changes into our lives. We can act out of fear and a lack of trust, which inevitably makes situations more difficult and has the potential to prolong our current circumstances. However, once we have the experience of coming through something difficult and realize that, despite outward appearances, the Lord was always working with our best interest at heart, we are able to let go and more readily trust Him. With this understanding, it becomes easier to allow Him to do a work that will greatly improve our lives. Even so, no matter how we act, the Lord will always respond to us with grace.

What does the Lord's grace look like in our everyday lives? Several years ago, I allowed a negative thought planted by the enemy to run wild in my head. Over time, it turned into a severe depression that lasted eight months.

Somehow, in the midst of the fog and confusion surrounding me, I was able to hold on to the Lord. In fact, I clung to Him for dear life. Every time a wave of fear or irrational thoughts hit me, I went to the Lord. Every time the enemy tried to shred my last remnants of hope, I cried out to the Lord, saying, "I need a miracle! I'm asking you to move heaven and earth on my behalf." And every time, the Lord brought wave after wave of grace through people to help me.

My family and my husband's family rallied around us. Longtime friends aided us. Numerous people offered their love and support during this difficult time. There was such an outpouring of grace from the Lord. The following were just a few experiences that help illustrate His grace in action.

Two very dear friends of mine from our house church group walked beside me. Although I tried to isolate myself, they reached out to me. One friend often had me over to her house for coffee to visit and made herself available to me day or night if I needed to talk. My other friend made CDs of encouraging spiritual music, watched my young children, and helped get me out of the house.

During this time, the Lord introduced me to a new friend. He prompted me to start attending a women's Bible study group at a nearby church where I ended up in a small group with this vibrant woman full of the Lord's Spirit. I felt drawn to her in some way.

Another woman in our group was going through a difficult time and was unable to stay composed. She was dealing with something that I had overcome in my life, and I felt a nudge from the Lord to speak into her life. The Lord used me and this vibrant woman to minister to this struggling sister. I never mentioned to anyone in our small group that I was battling depression. Actually, I felt a little better after helping this woman because I had stopped focusing on myself.

I continued going to the Bible study, but I didn't see the vibrant woman. A month later, she showed up again. At the end of the study, this woman walked up to me, introduced herself, and handed me an envelope with a card. My new friend wrote a very touching note saying how powerful it was to watch me minister to the women in our small group, especially the one who had been struggling. She also said that I was a powerful woman of God.

I cried as I read her card. I had become so focused on my own struggle with depression that I had started to identify myself as broken. She had only briefly met me once before, yet this woman was able to see through the depression to my true identity. I was touched that the Lord put it on her heart to reach out to me. I also had renewed hope that I was not as lost as I had feared.

I learned that my new friend ran a ministry to encourage women. A couple of weeks later, I was invited to my first event—a Valentine's party. At the party, my friend had people draw a piece of paper from a basket with a specific question about a struggle, challenge, or difficult circumstance they had overcome.

One by one, we took turns reading and then sharing the answers to our questions from our hearts. Two women received questions that covered issues that I was struggling with during my depression. I was awed and amazed by the honesty and transparency as both of them shared about how they had overcome the very same lies from the enemy that I was currently wrestling with.

I knew that it was no coincidence that both of these women were there and that they had each selected a question directly pertaining to me. The Lord had clearly done quite a bit of divine orchestrating on my behalf. I was deeply touched by His heart toward me.

As I drove home from the party, I was so moved that I cried tears of joy, pouring out my heart to God. This encounter was the impetus that I needed, and two weeks later, I found the courage to make the necessary changes to start the healing process.

The Lord used wave after wave of grace to chip away at the lie that entangled me in a web of depression. He didn't just magically make my problem disappear. I had created the problem, and I was going to have to work with the Lord to fix what I had done.

I had to take every thought captive. Each time a negative or destructive thought came into my mind, I had to replace it with something positive. I replaced those thoughts with a Bible verse, lyrics from a song, or specific words the Lord gave me for that season.

When going through a difficult period, most people want the Lord to immediately remove the problem from their lives. At times, the Lord supernaturally fixes the problem. More commonly, we see the potential for growth by walking through the experience with the Lord. Instead of instantly fixing the circumstances, the Lord pours out His grace to help sustain and guide you through to the other side.

This allows Him to transform, redeem, and restore you. You will ultimately come out of the situation a better person. The Lord will guide you and lead you through truth to equip you in an area that once bound you. He will set you free in that area of your life. As a result, you will learn empathy and the ability to recognize and speak into the lives of others who are going through the same experience.

God often works through people. If people are extending you grace and favor, the Lord is usually prompting them to do so. Recognizing the Lord's grace in our lives is just like communicating with Him. Once we are aware of the methods He uses to show us grace, we can recognize them more easily with each experience.

The Lord doesn't care how many times He has to extend grace to you about something or how many years it takes for you to hear Him. He is patient, and His end goal is for your good. Think of it in these terms. You know it will take ninety times for your child to figure out something life changing. Instead of having an attitude that says, "I've done this once, and now, I have to repeat it eighty-nine more times!" you would instead feel, "Yes, one experience done, and they are a step closer!"

Each interaction, no matter how seemingly irrelevant, is making progress and is also an encounter with the one you love. At His heart, the Lord's main desire is a relationship with us. Time spent with us is never wasted in His eyes. It is valuable and important for us both.

God Focuses on Forgiveness

Forgiveness is a key component of grace. God freely forgives us. Sometimes, the Lord asks us to extend grace to others by forgiving them. At times, we also need to forgive ourselves.

Forgiving someone is about you, not the other person. The only person unforgiveness hurts is yourself. It is the equivalent of you drinking poison and expecting the other person to be harmed. When you hold onto an offense, you inadvertently allow that offense to have a hold over you. Unforgiveness also gives the enemy access to you and your life.

You might have a valid reason to be upset or hurt by someone's actions, but it isn't worth your health. Forgiving them doesn't mean you have to stay friends with them or like their behavior or even them anymore. Forgiving them doesn't mean that you are pretending it didn't happen.

When you forgive someone, you are releasing them to God. You make a conscious decision that your freedom and well-being are more important than holding onto a grudge. Unforgiveness can hinder the flow of God's grace in your life. Forgiveness gives God's grace access to heal both of your lives.

Sometimes, the person we need to forgive is ourselves. When we mess up, we are tempted to turn inwards. If not checked, guilt and shame can run rampant and keep us trapped in an unhealthy cycle of self-condemnation. When we condemn ourselves, we are judging our own lives, which we do not have the authority to do. During self-condemnation, we will either subconsciously or intentionally deny ourselves the grace the Lord offers us.

God went to great lengths to set us free in every way. He forgave mankind for every transgression from the beginning of time until the end of time. The last thing He wants us to do is to go back under the very thing from which He freed us. As expressed by C.S. Lewis, "I think that if God forgives us we must forgive ourselves. Otherwise, it is almost like setting up ourselves as a higher tribunal than Him."[21]

Grace is a freely given, divine gift that it is not corruptible. It is all-encompassing and everlasting. It is God's unique gift of love to mankind born out of His ultimate sacrifice for us. It enables us to live the life that He has destined for us. And finally, as expressed by the Apostle Paul, "But by the grace of God I am what I am, and his grace toward me was not in vain" (1 Corinthians 15:10, ESV).

---

[21] Lewis, W.H. and Hooper, Walter, eds. 1993. *The Letters of C.S. Lewis*. New York, NY: Harper Collins.

Thank You for Purchasing This Book

Thank you for taking the time to read this book. Your input is a valuable tool to help me with future books. I would appreciate it if you take a moment to write a review on Amazon and provide me with helpful feedback.

Tanya Vezza

www.ingramcontent.com/pod-product-compliance
Lightning Source LLC
Chambersburg PA
CBHW061329040426
42444CB00011B/2830